THE

SINNER'S

PRAYER

FACT OR FICTION?

◄ANDREW STROM

RevivalSchool

THE SINNER'S PRAYER – FACT OR FICTION?

Published by: RevivalSchool
www.revivalschool.com

Wholesale distribution by Lightning Source, Inc.

Scripture taken from the New King James Version®. Copyright © 1982 by Thomas Nelson, Inc. Used by permission. All rights reserved.

[Sometimes the KJV is also quoted].

ISBN-13: 978-0-9831866-1-8

ISBN-10: 0-9831866-1-8

CONTENTS

CHAPTER ONE

THE LOST FOUNDATIONS

SCENARIO ONE

A 17 year old young man, feeling a bit down, attends a Youth event at a local church fellowship. He is told that only Christ can give him the fulfillment in life that he craves. He agrees to "give Jesus a try". The youth pastor sits down and leads him in a sinner's prayer – where he is told to simply repeat the words that are fed to him line by line – accepting Jesus as his "Lord and savior" and inviting Christ "into his heart". The youth pastor then claps him on the back, exclaiming with a wide grin, "Welcome to the kingdom of God! You are now saved! You are now a born again Christian! How does it feel?" The young man doesn't truly know how to respond, but he grins and assumes he must now "have it" – this Christianity that he is wanting to try out. He buys himself a Bible, makes an effort to pray for a few minutes each day, and attends church regularly for several months. But he is not finding it quite as "fulfilling" as he had hoped, and there still seems to be a yawning spiritual gulf in his life that remains unquenched. After a number of months he gradually drifts away – yet another statistic - to join the growing thousands who have "tried Jesus" in similar fashion and then slowly slipped out the back door.

SCENARIO TWO

A middle-aged woman is invited by a friend to an evangelistic crusade being held at the church fellowship down the street. The preacher is on top form - very compelling and persuasive. He tells her that Christ will meet her every need and solve all her problems in this life – as well as reserving her a place in heaven in the next. The choir sings beautifully. She feels almost tearful as the music swells and the "altar call" is given. Along with perhaps 20 others she makes her way down the front – where she is assigned a "counselor" and taken to a back room. Just like the 17-year-old she is led in a sinner's prayer in which she "gives her heart to the Lord". She repeats the words line by line, just as she is told. She feels a slight warmth inside – and feels sure she is doing the right thing. The counselor congratulates her fulsomely, asking her to write her details on a printed form and giving her a "follow-up pack" to take home.

Over ensuing months she gets more and more involved with the fellowship – the coffee mornings, the fund-raisers, the food-bank. She feels her life has taken a definite turn for the better. She is not exactly what you would call "on fire" for God, but she does pray occasionally and read her Bible – as well as tithing and attending church every week. She feels very happy with her new-found Christian friends and her new-found Christian life.

ARE THESE PEOPLE TRULY "SAVED"?

Many Christians will be shocked that we are even asking this question. "Of course they are saved!" they will say. "They prayed the sinner's prayer – they gave their heart to the Lord. Isn't that what the Bible tells us to do?"

Ah - a very good question. "Isn't that what the Bible tells us to do?" A truly worthwhile question indeed, as it turns out.

But there is no doubt that we in the church think this is one question that we truly have a handle on. We really do think we know the answer. After all, we have been brought up with it our entire church lives, have we not?

Personally, from my earliest church days I simply assumed that the Sinner's Prayer was a biblical fact. From my infancy onwards I was brought up in various forms of mainstream evangelicalism – from the Open Brethren and the Baptists through to the Assemblies of God. And as a young adult I got involved with the Navigators and Campus Crusade for Christ. All of them seemed to preach the same thing. It was simply unquestioned. The Sinner's Prayer was the "Bible" way of becoming converted. Everybody knew that. Who ever thought any different?

It was only later after I was truly converted myself that I began to search the Bible and unearth some increasingly disturbing questions. And the more I searched, the more concerned I became.

Here are some examples of the kinds of questions that began to hit me full-force:-

(1) If the "little prayer" method is correct, then why don't we ever see ANY apostle or ANY evangelist in the whole New Testament telling someone to do this to be saved?

(2) And when the apostles did tell someone how to be converted, why was it utterly different to what we tell people today?

(3) And when we see in the Bible thousands being saved and entire groups being converted, why are NONE of them being led in a "Sinner's Prayer" or anything like it?

(4) And in fact, when we go searching through the Bible for this whole "Give your heart to the Lord"/ Sinner's Prayer thing, why does it not even seem to EXIST in Scripture? (And yes – for those who object to what I am saying, your objections will certainly be covered in this book. But I bet you will be surprised at how flimsy many of these objections appear under closer examination).

THE SHOCKING IMPLICATIONS

The fact is, the modern church has gone right around the globe preaching the Sinner's Prayer. Over the years I have ministered in many nations and I tell you, this teaching is worldwide – from Denmark to South Africa, from Australia to Nigeria, from the UK to the USA. It is totally global. And for a lot of people, their entire salvation stands or falls upon it. But what if it is little less than a cheap, watered-down placebo? What if it is simply another product of our instant "drive-thru" culture? A kind of McSalvation to get people into our modern McChurch? What if the "little prayer" was invented not by Jesus or the apostles, but rather by gospel cheapeners over the last 70 years or so – simply to make the process of "salvation" more convenient? What if (horror of horrors) we were to turn it over and find the plastic words "Made in Taiwan" written large underneath?

The tragedy and seriousness of it all is that right around the globe, this is the very thing that multitudes have been told will save them. "Simply pray this little prayer after me," the preacher says. "Just repeat these words, accepting Jesus into your heart, and you will be saved." And so millions upon millions around the world have obeyed, and now their entire salvation stands or falls on whether this little two-minute procedure is true or false. Don't you find that alarming? I know I do.

It is important to note here that people's experiences in praying this prayer often differ quite widely. For every person who senses almost nothing at all, you can always find others who deeply meant everything they prayed. And in these cases there can certainly be genuine heartfelt repentance, deep surrender, and real, lasting change. This greatly depends, not on "repeating the prayer" itself, but on what has gone on beforehand. If there has been a long process of conviction or God's dealings in a person's life, then the "little prayer" can become something much more than just the sum of its parts. However, sadly there are also huge numbers of people for whom it is a very shallow experience indeed – and this may well be because it is simply not truly biblical! (As we shall see). In this sense it could almost be viewed as an "accident" when something deeper comes out of it. And the raw statistics of modern evangelism certainly seem to bear this out.

In his excellent book, *Hell's Best Kept Secret*, Ray Comfort makes the point that modern evangelism is often so sadly ineffective that it boasts only a 20 percent holding rate. He also quotes one evangelistic campaign involving 178 churches in which only three percent of the converts remained! "How effective are our present-day evangelical methods," he asks, "when they create eighty backsliders for every one hundred 'decisions for Jesus'? Some are even less effective than that," he continues. "One recent campaign reported having a 92 percent backsliding rate!" *(- 'Hell's Best-Kept Secret,'* Page 1).

But it is not only those who backslide that are the problem. Many who remain in our churches, faithfully attending week after week, are clearly in a very similar predicament. I was once told by an evangelical pastor in the American Midwest that he doubted whether more than five percent of his congregation were truly saved. And yet they are mostly God-believing "respectable" people who faithfully attend church every week! But attending church and assenting to all the beliefs & creeds is not what saves us, is it? It is an inwardly transformed life. It is being made an utterly "new creation" in Him. It is radical discipleship of the kind that only Jesus can produce.

The famous preacher Leonard Ravenhill once declared, "I doubt that more than two percent of professing Christians in the United States are truly born again." A deeply shocking statement – but could it be true? And if it is true, might you be numbered among that two percent, my friend?

Many apparently believe that all you need to do is "pray the little prayer," then try to be a "nice" person, go to church, pay your tithes, etc, and all will be well with you on Judgment Day. But how can such thinking be tallied with the Bible in any way? Jesus clearly stated: "**If anyone desires to come after me, let him deny himself, and take up his cross, and follow me**" (Mt 16:24). Does that sound cheap and convenient to you? He also said: "Enter by the narrow gate; for wide is the gate and broad is the way that leads to destruction, and there are many who go in by it. Because narrow is the gate and difficult is the way which leads to life, and there are few who find it" (Mt 7:13-14).

True "Bible" Christianity involves radical discipleship. And that in turn requires a radically powerful conversion. Today's quick and easy "pray a little prayer" conversions are not only unbiblical, but they often lead to a Christianity utterly lacking in power and true transformation. Sadly, shallow conversions beget shallow believers. A lukewarm gospel begets a lukewarm church. This is totally predictable. And God is calling us away from it all - back to the original powerful gospel and the original powerful conversion experience – where new converts take off like a rocket ship – desiring to be full disciples from day one. There was never any such thing as a "mediocre" conversion in the Bible. They were always powerful and utterly life-transforming. And so it must be again in our day.

Friend, please take the time to ask yourself the following questions about the state of your own soul:-

Am I a true disciple, or mostly just a church-goer? Have I had a powerful conversion experience where I was utterly transformed in the inner man? Is it "Christ in me, the hope of glory?" Was the transformation so great that it is truly no longer I that live, but Christ that lives in me? Is my conscience clean, are my robes washed in His blood, am I truly a "new creation" in Him? Do I experience these things every day as a tangible reality in my life?

This is the type of conversion that happened daily and hourly in the New Testament – and it is what we must get back to. And that, hopefully, is what this book is all about.

THE LOST FOUNDATIONS

If you asked many Christians today what are the "foundations" or 'elementary teachings' about Christ that need to be laid in every new believer's life – you may get a number of different answers. Some will guess most of these basic elements correctly, but many will leave out some of the most vital ones – since we hardly hear them preached as such today. Fortunately the Scriptures do not leave us guessing as to what these basic foundations are. They are spelled out for us in Hebrews 6:1-2 – a passage that every gospel preacher in the world should know back-to-front. But sadly it seems that many today do not.

As you go through this book, you will notice that in almost every chapter there is found at least one "Mini Bible Study". I cannot emphasize strongly enough how important these little Bible Studies are to gain an understanding of the whole "Sinner's Prayer" topic. Please don't skip past them. They are designed to take only minutes to complete – and the understanding you will gain from them is utterly crucial to the topic we are discussing. It is highly doubtful that anyone who skips these Bible Studies will come to grips with this book very well at all. The first of them – on the "six foundations" of Hebrews 6 - is below:

MINI BIBLE STUDY - ESSENTIAL

Please look up each Scripture and write your answers to the questions below (or on another sheet of paper if you wish)-

(a) READ Heb 6:1-2. Then write out the "six foundations" below (numbering them)-

ANSWER – (1)_____

(2)_____

(3)_____

(4)_____

(5)_____

(6)_____

(b) How important do you think these six things are?

ANSWER - _____

(c) What words does verse 1 use to describe these six things?

ANSWER - _____

(d) In building and construction, what happens if the foundations are not laid correctly?

ANSWER - _____

BACK TO FIRST PRINCIPLES

We have now taken our first look at what the King James Version calls the "principles of the doctrine of Christ". These six things – Repentance, Faith, Baptisms, Laying on of hands, Resurrection from the dead, and Eternal Judgment – surely have to be considered the most crucial foundations that must be laid in every believer's life. And yet, in many cases today they are not. Don't you think this might be one of the major reasons for the mess we are in?

Please notice that there is no mention at all amongst these First Principles of "Accepting Jesus into your heart" or repeating some kind of "rote prayer" to be saved. If it were up to modern preachers, this would have been the first thing on the list. It would have been- "(1) Say a prayer asking Jesus into your heart" or something similar. Isn't it strange that it is nowhere to be seen? (And not for the last time!)

As we shall see, time and time again where a modern Christian would expect to see the Sinner's Prayer being used in the Bible, it is simply not there. In fact, after studying and studying these passages throughout the New Testament, I personally came to the conclusion that this "Ask Jesus into your heart" doctrine simply DOES NOT EXIST in Scripture. I know that is shocking to a lot of people, but it is simply the conclusion I was forced to come to.

Some claim that "repentance and faith" are the same as "Asking Jesus into your heart." I am sorry, but scripturally that doesn't ring true at all (as we shall see in the next chapter). True repentance and true faith in the Bible were not the same as repeating some little rote prayer that takes about two minutes to recite. I mean, how could we even claim such a thing?

Much of this book will be spent going on an adventure through the Scriptures, discovering for ourselves the truth of this matter. Yes – the implications are shocking. But that is even more reason to get to the bottom of it. We are talking here about one of the most basic practices of the modern church around the world. And if it is error, it is a very tragic and serious matter indeed.

So what, then, did the apostles preach when they were trying to get someone converted? Is it possible that instead of the Sinner's Prayer they used the Hebrews 6 "Foundations" instead? Rather than "Asking Jesus into your heart," was it more a foundation of Repentance, Faith, Baptisms, Laying on of hands, Resurrection from the dead, and Eternal Judgment that they were seeking to establish in peoples' lives in these Bible conversions? Just what exactly was the true apostolic pattern? Over the next few chapters, that is exactly what we will be attempting to find out.

CHAPTER TWO

A 'BELIEF' THAT DOES NOT SAVE

Before we go any further, I think it is important that we talk briefly about "Bible" repentance and "Bible" faith, since these are such crucial components of any true conversion. And not only that, but they are the first of the Foundations that we just saw listed in Hebrews chapter 6.

What is true Repentance? Many people have a rather vague impression of what this word truly means – but there is a great deal of information about it in Scripture. For instance we are told in the Gospels that the preacher who came 'preparing the way' for Jesus had an entire ministry that revolved around Repentance. This, of course, was John the Baptist – and what a piercing, convicting message he brought! Publicly denouncing sin, hypocrisy and worldliness wherever he found it – this was the bold and fiery preaching of a "forerunner" prophet sent by God. And he laid the platform for much of the preaching that followed.

So how did people respond to John's message? The Bible says that he came "preaching a baptism of repentance for the remission of sins" (Lk 3:3). And what did people do when they came to be baptized? Matthew 3:6 tells us that they "were baptized by him in the Jordan, confessing their sins." Yes – confession of sins to God was a big part of repentance. Which is exactly what we would expect, since the Bible tells us that, "If we confess our sins, He is faithful and just to forgive us our sins and to cleanse us from all unrighteousness" (1 Jn 1:9).

But true Repentance is not just about confession of sins – because sometimes people can do that in quite a mechanical, ritualistic way. They are not pierced to the depths of their soul by what they have done. True "Bible" repentance involves what the Scriptures call "godly sorrow" – a deep, Holy Spirit-led mourning for the sins we have committed. "For godly sorrow produces repentance leading to salvation…" (2 Cor 7:10). That is why true Repentance preaching must pierce us to the very core of our being.

Probably the best example that Jesus gives of true repentance is found in Luke 18:13- "And the tax collector, standing afar off, would not so much as raise his eyes to heaven, but beat his breast, saying, 'God, be merciful to me a sinner!'"

The Greek word for Repentance is "metanoia" – literally "a change of mind". It is a complete change of heart and mind about sin – a deep humbling and "turning away" that involves godly sorrow, confession of sins and a permanently changed life. The very first word out of Jesus' mouth was the word "Repent". He simply took up where John the Baptist left off – as did the apostles throughout the New Testament. And we need to continue following their example in our own day.

But sadly it is becoming more and more rare in the church today to find true Repentance preached – or experienced by the people. Many preachers seem very reluctant to preach searchingly or convictingly about sin. Perhaps they are afraid of "offending" someone – or losing people from their congregation. And so the church limps on in an unsaved twilight zone for want of a few good men. The foundations of the faith are simply no longer being laid in people's lives.

WHAT IS TRUE BIBLE FAITH?

When I lived in California, a team of us used to travel into Los Angeles to minister to the homeless on Skid Row. Tragically, the vast majority of them were on crack cocaine, heroin or similar drugs. Many were involved in theft, violence, selling their bodies or drug-dealing. And yet it was a blessing to be there, ministering mercy to the outcasts and all who were "oppressed of the devil." But I was often amazed to find that many already considered themselves to be "saved Christians" – even while high on drugs, full of darkness and utter depravity. If you asked them, "Do you believe in Jesus?" they would answer, "Yes, of course." And yet it was a 'belief' that changed nothing. They merely "believed" it without living it in any way. A lot of them even claimed to be 'born again' because they had prayed the Sinner's Prayer at some point in their past. The fact that their lives were filled with utter darkness and degradation didn't even seem to enter the equation. There is not the slightest bit of biblical support for such a theory, of course. You cannot claim the light of Jesus and go live like the devil. In fact, the exact opposite is true. (See 1 Cor 6:9-10 and Gal 5:19-21).

When I look at the Scriptures it seems to me that we should perhaps make some kind of distinction between "full" faith and what I call "head-belief". There are those who have truly experienced the full faith of the gospel – a deep, life-transforming faith that only Christ can give. And then there are others who have heard the gospel and agreed with it – but have yet to fully obey or experience its power. These are seemingly in a state of "head-faith" only. They have a genuine "belief" of a kind, but it has not yet transmitted itself into the full 'heart' faith that we see in the New Testament. Their lives have yet to be truly transformed by what they have heard.

The Bible says: "For by grace you have been saved through faith, and that not of yourselves; it is the gift of God..." (Eph 2:8). There you have it. True faith is a GIFT from God. It is not something that man can generate within himself. True faith is "supernatural". It is birthed from above in the heart of man. It is a gift that we must EXPERIENCE. And sadly there are too many in our world today who seem to have some kind of "belief" yet who have never experienced this glorious infusion from the King of Kings.

Let's take a look at one of the most famous Scriptures on Faith in the whole Bible. "But without faith it is impossible to please Him, for he who comes to God must believe that He is, and that He is a rewarder of those who diligently seek Him" (Heb 11:6). Isn't it tragic that we have so many in the world today who "believe that

God is" and yet utterly fail to "diligently seek Him"? It is like they have 'half' a faith. And if we go by this Scripture then sadly we must conclude that half a faith is really no faith at all.

This is why we need to be so careful to define what we mean when we tell people to "only believe" and talk about "the faith that alone saves us." We must define what true faith is. We must tell them that it is a supernatural gift from God – a deep, abiding, life-transforming infusion from above – not some "half-faith" that leaves us still in our sins and utterly untransformed. This is exactly the kind of thing that the apostle James was warning of when he wrote: "You believe that there is one God. You do well. Even the devils believe – and tremble! But do you want to know, O foolish man, that faith without works is dead?" (James 2:19-20). Notice the "two types" of faith that James is speaking of here. One is a living, active faith while the other is a 'dead' belief that produces no fruit.

FAITH IN WHAT?

Since the Bible shows us that true faith is "supernatural" in origin, what exactly should we experience when God implants this divine gift into our lives? Well, obviously our faith is to be centered on Christ and what He has done for us. And so this divine gift will enable us to deeply "trust" Jesus and His imputed righteousness for our salvation. In other words, this supernatural faith will enable us to actually "experience" Christ's righteousness living inside us – as though it was our own. A sense of "clean-ness" and true "peace with God" will be the result. By abiding in this faith we will actually know and experience the purity of Jesus living on the inside. And as we keep our conscience clean before Him, we can actually "walk" in these pure white robes before God, "washed in the blood of the Lamb." Sadly, only a minority of church people today seem to experience this true Faith of the Bible as an actual reality in their lives. It is supposed to be constant and never leave us.

In today's world it is said that 80% of Americans claim to be born-again Christians – half of them living like complete heathens all the while. Is such a "half-faith" of any value to God? Does He think it's

OK simply to claim "belief" while living exactly how you want? No, of course not. Of such folly is the wide road to destruction paved. The Bible makes this very clear – over and over again.

But sadly even our evangelical churches today are riddled with this exact same dilemma:- People who have prayed the Sinner's Prayer and yet live for themselves the vast majority of the time. People who claim a "belief" in Jesus and yet remain completely untransformed. People who believe that "God is" and yet utterly fail to "diligently seek Him." A twilight faith, a half-conversion, a sub-salvation that is no salvation at all. And it results in an army of "nice" respectable church-going folk who show virtually no sign of the deep work of the cross in their lives. I think it is high time the church starts to once again preach a Faith that actually saves, before Jesus returns and a whole lot of half-preachers of half-gospels find themselves in the worst possible predicament before Him.

IN CONCLUSION

So there we have it. A discussion of the first two "foundations". And I'm sure a lot of people are largely in agreement. There is not too much controversy about insisting that true Repentance and true Faith are both essential. But now we are about to head into more controversial waters. In coming chapters we will be exploring the Book of Acts to see how exactly the apostles got people converted. And for a lot of us I believe some real surprises are in store.

CHAPTER THREE

OUTPOURING IN JERUSALEM

Earlier we raised the question of whether we see the apostles using the Hebrews 6 "Foundations" when getting people converted – or whether we see them using something like our modern "Sinner's prayer". Of course, this is an extremely vital question. And there is no doubt that the first place we should look for an answer is in the Book of Acts. Why? Simply because Acts is the only "history" that we have of the early years of the church. It is called the "Acts of the Apostles" after all. And in it we see literally thousands of people becoming converted and entire groups coming to the Lord. So it is an ideal place to start.

Now, the first time we see one of these mass-conversions is on the Day of Pentecost. As most of us know, this was the day, right at the start of Acts, when the Holy Spirit was first outpoured and the Church itself was born. As such it has to be one of the most momentous days in world history. And the crowd that gathered to hear Peter preach that day were a very interesting mix of people.

The Bible tells us that staying in Jerusalem at that time were devout Jews from all over the known world. Obviously many of them had come because of the celebration of Pentecost – which was a major feast on the Jewish calendar. So all these practising Jews were gathered in one place – including those who lived in Jerusalem itself.

And what did the apostle Peter preach to this assembled multitude? He went right for the jugular! Utterly fearless, Peter preached one of the most convicting sermons ever recorded in Scripture. He accused them of crucifying the very Messiah that they had been waiting for all these years. (This was simply the most awful thing that a devout Jew could imagine doing). Yes – they had killed their true Messiah - the Christ - and now He had been exalted to the right hand of God.

This was the most terrifying and piercing thing that these people had ever heard. What sinners they were! Murdering the very Messiah sent from God! The Scripture records that they were "cut to the heart" by what Peter told them, and cried out asking what they could do to be forgiven.

And now comes an opportunity to take our first look at how people were converted under the apostles' ministry. Please complete the Mini Bible Study below – which takes a close look at what happened. This is very important-

MINI BIBLE STUDY - ESSENTIAL

Please look up each Scripture and write your answers to the questions below (or on another sheet of paper if you wish)-

(a) READ Acts 2:37-38. What were the 3 components of Peter's answer when they cried, "What shall we do?" (Please number them)-

ANSWER – (1)_____

(2)_____

(3)_____

(b) Please read on through verse 41. Do we see any signs of the people saying a "sinner's prayer" or giving their "heart to the Lord" in this entire passage?

ANSWER - _____

(c) How soon did they baptize them?

ANSWER - _____

(d) Do you think this is the kind of place that we might expect the Sinner's Prayer to show up if the apostles used such a thing? Why?

ANSWER - _____

(e) What do you think a modern preacher might say today if some non-Christians asked him the question, "Men and brothers, what shall we do?"

ANSWER - _____

(f) Finally, just as a reminder, please write out again the "six foundations" of Hebrews 6:1-2:

ANSWER - _____

OUR FIRST LOOK AT THE APOSTOLIC PATTERN

There is no question that the answer Peter gave in Acts 2:38 is remarkably different from what the modern church would give today. Have you ever heard a modern preacher tell someone that they needed to (1) Repent, (2) be Baptized, and (3) Receive the Holy Spirit? And have you ever seen them go and baptize that person the very same hour?

I can just picture it now. The modern evangelist in his flashy three-piece suit with the soulful choir chiming in behind. The "altar call" awash with emotion-laden music. "I see that hand," comes the call. "Just repeat this little prayer after me and you will be saved." It just doesn't bear comparison, does it? The conversion experience that those people went through on the Day of Pentecost almost couldn't be more different. So how on earth did we end up today with a conversion method that is so utterly different from Pentecost?

But perhaps, you may be thinking, this was just a one-off example. Perhaps they didn't always use the "foundations" in converting people. Perhaps we still may find somewhere in the Book of Acts where the apostles actually told people to "Ask Jesus into their heart" after all.

Well, the world loves an optimist. So let us carry on with our exploration and see if this same pattern plays itself out in the rest of Acts or not.

CHAPTER FOUR

REVIVAL & MIRACLES IN SAMARIA

There is actually quite an interesting pattern found in the Book of Acts. Jesus had told His disciples, "You shall be witnesses to Me in Jerusalem, and in all Judea and Samaria, and to the end of the earth" (Acts 1:8b). And it certainly seems that the chronology of reaching these various people-groups did indeed follow this pattern.

The Revival in Jerusalem was a massive one, with multiplied thousands of converts in just a matter of days. This powerful move of God obviously went on for some time in the Judea region. And then the very next people-group that we see being reached were the Samaritans.

The city and region of Samaria was not too far removed from Jerusalem. But there had been a lot of bitterness and enmity between the Jews and Samaritans over many years. One of the reasons for this was that the Samaritans were not seen as true Israelites, but rather something of a "mixed multitude". This was because after the invasion of the Assyrians around 721 BC, most of the Israelites in Samaria had gone away into captivity while other nationalities had been brought in to replace them. Many of these gradually intermarried with the remaining Israelites, and slowly came to worship the One True God of the Hebrews. But they were never fully accepted as true Israelites.

Jesus, however, did extend to them a large degree of acceptance – and they seemed to accept Him also. And when the time came for Christianity to explode throughout the entire country and region, they became one of the most responsive groups ever to hear the gospel.

It is in Acts chapter 8 that we first read of Philip the evangelist going down to preach in Samaria. And it seems that almost immediately a huge Revival broke out. There were many miraculous healings and demons came out of many who were possessed, "crying with a loud voice." The lame walked, the blind could see, and the city was filled with joy.

Again, like in Jerusalem, this was a situation where we see "mass-conversion" taking place. So what actually happened when these people were converted? Let's take a look! Below is a Mini Bible Study on this topic. Please complete it if at all possible:

MINI BIBLE STUDY - ESSENTIAL

As always, please look up each Scripture and write your answers to the questions below-

(a) Please READ Acts 8:12-17. Again, in this passage, do we see people "asking Jesus into their heart" or "praying a little prayer" like we do today?

ANSWER - _____

(b) Like Pentecost, there seemed to be 3 important elements in the conversion of the Samaritans. What were these 3 things?

*ANSWER – (1)*_____

*(2)*_____

*(3)*_____

(c) How soon were they baptized?

ANSWER – _____

(d) What was the "laying on of hands" for?

ANSWER – _____

(e) Does it seem to you that the New Testament evangelists and apostles were again using the Hebrews 6 "foundations" here, rather than the "sinner's prayer" in converting people to Christ?

ANSWER - _____

IS A PATTERN STARTING TO EMERGE?

We have now examined the first two mass-conversions detailed in the Book of Acts – conversions that involved literally thousands of people getting saved. So even at this early stage, is it possible to discern the beginnings of an "apostolic pattern" developing?

In the Acts 8 account that we just looked at, it seemed that the three components described in the conversions were- (1) Believing, (2) Being baptized, and (3) The "laying on of hands" to receive the Holy Spirit. Meanwhile, in the 'Pentecost' account that we looked at in the last chapter, the three components that Peter preached were- (1) Repentance, (2) Baptism, and (3) Receiving the Holy Spirit.

Obviously these patterns are very similar to one another – though there is one significant difference. In Samaria it does not tell us specifically that they "repented". Should we then assume that these people did not repent, or is it a case where it was simply not described in the account that we have? It doesn't seem to make sense that they might become converted without repenting, does it? But anyway, one thing is sure: In neither of these accounts do we see anything like "Asking Jesus into your heart" or 'Repeating a little prayer' to be saved.

Let's not be hasty, though. Couldn't it still be a little soon to write-off the Sinner's Prayer just yet? We still have a number of accounts in the Book of Acts to look at, so let's continue to give it a decent chance. But it sure isn't looking good, is it? Thousands of people converted already and still no sign of it anywhere.

For a doctrine that is preached around the world today, it will be very serious indeed if it is not found preached in the book of Acts. A huge dilemma for the church. So we still have some important exploration to do.

CHAPTER FIVE

THE CONVERSION OF SAUL

It is in the very next chapter of Acts (chapter 9) that we first read about the conversion of Saul (who later became the apostle Paul). At this time Saul was still quite a young man – and yet more and more he was becoming one of the most severe instigators of persecution against the early church.

It all seemed to start with the stoning of Stephen (Acts 7) during which those who were doing the stoning had laid their clothes at Saul's feet while they went about their ugly business. After that, it seemed, Saul hardened his heart and set his course for the destruction of Christianity more and more.

In Acts 8 we are told that he "made havoc of the church, entering every house, and dragging off men and women, committing them to prison" (Acts 8:3). He had become one of the harshest persecutors of the church in her short history.

And so, in Acts chapter 9 we find Saul on his way to Damascus, still "breathing threats and murder against the disciples of the Lord." And yet this time it was he who was about to get the shock of his life.

Of course we all know the story. A blinding light from heaven suddenly shone all around him. He fell to the ground and heard a voice speaking to him – "Saul, Saul, why are you persecuting me?" It was the voice of Jesus – the very One whose beloved church he had been attacking. A blind and trembling Saul was led by his friends into Damascus to await further instructions from the Lord.

So was this the moment at which Saul became truly converted? A lot of people seem to think so. They think that when he was stunned by the blinding light and heard the voice of Jesus – this must have been the moment at which he was truly "born again". But was this, in fact, the case? What does the Bible actually tell us? What clues do we have?

Below is a Mini Bible Study that seeks to answer these very questions. Please complete it if you are able:

MINI BIBLE STUDY - ESSENTIAL

As always, please look up each Scripture and write your answers to the questions below (or on another sheet of paper)-

(a) Please READ Acts 9:3-18. After reading the whole passage, does it seem to you that Saul was fully converted on the Damascus Road, or more likely after Ananias was sent to minister to him in Damascus? Give reasons for your answer:

ANSWER – _____

_____

(b) Do we see (1) Repentance, (2) Baptism and (3) Receiving the Holy Spirit in this passage?

ANSWER – _____

(c) In verse 17, does it seem that Saul received the Holy Spirit through the "laying on of hands"?

ANSWER – _____

(d) In this case, did it seem to matter too much what ORDER baptism or the infilling of the Spirit occurred?

ANSWER – _____

In Acts 22 we find another account of Saul's conversion, in which we learn more details about his baptism. Please READ Acts 16:22. After reading this verse, do you think Saul had had his "sins washed away" earlier when he saw the blinding light – or only now upon being baptized?

ANSWER – _____

In that case, when do you believe he became fully converted?

ANSWER – _____

THE SURPRISES KEEP ON COMING

It almost goes without saying, of course, that we still do not see the slightest sign of "Asking Jesus into your heart" or anything similar in the conversion of Saul. But on the other hand, it certainly seems that we ARE starting to see a familiar pattern being repeated over and over again. What is that pattern? (1) Repentance, (2) Faith, (3) Baptism, and (4) Receiving the Holy Spirit (often through the "laying on of hands"). How could we not see this as a direct correlation with the 'foundations' of Hebrews 6?

Of course, a lot of people will be surprised at what we are now noticing about the conversion of Saul. It has become almost a received fact in many circles that he became "born again" during his 'blinding light' experience on the Damascus road. But no – this cannot be. There is no way that Ananias would be saying to a truly born-again person, "Arise and be baptized, and WASH AWAY YOUR SINS, calling on the name of the Lord" (Acts 22:16). If he had not yet had his sins washed away (which clearly he hadn't, according to this Scripture), then there was no way that he was yet truly converted or "born again". Don't you think this is a fair conclusion?

The fact is, if you are a proponent of the Sinner's Prayer or "Giving your heart to the Lord," then Saul's conversion becomes an enormous problem. There is simply no way of reading Acts 22:16 (above) without being confronted with the fact of how important baptism is, and how lacking in evidence your own position seems to be. And sad to say, it is only going to get worse – not better – as we continue our exploration through the Book of Acts. By now the jury must surely be nearing its verdict. But again, it is unfair to come to a conclusion on such an important issue while using only partial evidence. So let the investigation continue!

CHAPTER SIX

OUTPOURING UPON THE GENTILES

The very next people-group that we see being reached in the Book of Acts is a group of "godly Gentiles". However, it took quite a lot before Peter even wanted to have anything to do with them!

You see, the Gentiles (or non-Jews) were seen as ceremonially "unclean" in Jewish culture. You could not eat with them or enter their homes, or any such thing. This was simply the way that Peter had been brought up. So how did God overcome such an attitude, when He wanted Peter to go and preach to the Gentiles for the very first time?

In Acts 10 we find Peter on a housetop near the city of Joppa praying. Suddenly God shows him a vision of all kinds of 'unclean' beasts and animals. A voice says to him, "Rise, Peter; kill and eat." Peter refuses, because the beasts are unclean. But he is shown the vision three times, and each time the voice says to him, "What God has cleansed you must not call unclean."

The next thing, three men arrive from the household of Cornelius the Roman centurion, asking that Peter might come and preach to his household. Cornelius had seen a vision of an angel commanding him to do this. Cornelius is described in Scripture as "a devout man and one who feared God with all his household, who gave alms generously to the people, and prayed to God always (Acts 10:2). After the vision that Peter has just experienced, he had little hesitation in accompanying the men. The first Gentile encounter was underway!

It is important to note that up until this time, the only people-groups who had experienced the gospel were basically Jews and Samaritans – so this was a big departure. What do we see happening, then, when this first group of Gentiles becomes truly converted?

The following Mini Bible Study will help us find out. Please complete it if you are able:

MINI BIBLE STUDY - ESSENTIAL

As usual, please look up each Scripture and write your answers to the questions below-

(a) READ Acts 10:44-48. Is the pattern here similar to what we have seen in the other passages? In what way?

ANSWER - _____

_____

(b) Do you think the fact that these people were already godly, holiness-seeking people made a difference in why they received the Holy Spirit so readily? Give reasons for your answer.

ANSWER - _____

(c) How did the onlookers know that these people were filled with the Holy Spirit?

ANSWER - _____

(d) Was it "optional" for them to be baptized?

ANSWER - _____

(e) When Peter says in verse 47 that they "have received the Holy Spirit just as we have," it seems obvious that he is referring to his own experience on the Day of Pentecost. Please READ Acts 2:4. What are the similarities that you can see?

ANSWER - _____

_____

(f) Please READ Acts 11:15-18 where Peter is later describing what happened with Cornelius' household. When you compare this passage with Acts 10:44-48 and also Acts 2:4 - does it seem that being "filled with", 'baptized with', or "receiving" the Holy Spirit may all refer to the same experience? Quote Scripture to back up your answer.

ANSWER - _____

_____

_____

(g) Also, in light of these passages, do you think that the Spirit "coming upon" or "falling upon" someone is generally referring to this same type of experience?

ANSWER - _____

GRIM NEWS FOR THE LITTLE PRAYER

Needless to say, once again, the whole approach of "repeating a little prayer" to be saved is nowhere to be seen in the conversion of the godly Gentiles. And neither has it been so much as glimpsed in any of the conversions that we have studied. The news is indeed looking grim for the modern Sinner's Prayer.

But the above account is interesting for a lot of other reasons also. For the first time we are able to see how the apostles used the terms "Receiving" the Holy Spirit, "Baptism" of the Spirit, "Filled" with the Spirit, the Holy Spirit "coming upon" someone, etc. And interestingly, we see all these terms seemingly applied interchangeably. That is probably news to a lot of people. But I can tell you, when you study the use of these same terms right the way through the New Testament, you end up coming to the same conclusion. This is particularly obvious in the above passages from Acts 10 and 11. "Receiving" or being 'Filled' or being "Baptized" with the Holy Spirit are all exactly the same thing in the Bible.

Another point that we should take note of is that once these Gentiles had received the Holy Spirit, Peter actually COMMANDED that they be baptized in water also. It was not an "optional" thing. It was seemingly treated as a commandment of God at that point. I wonder how many believers there are around the world today who have been filled with the Holy Spirit, and yet have never bothered to obey Jesus in water-baptism? Hopefully we are now starting to see what a serious issue this really is.

CHAPTER SEVEN

REVIVAL AMONGST THE EPHESIANS

In Acts 19 we find another very interesting people-group being reached by the apostles. This time it was some disciples of John the Baptist that Paul discovered in Ephesus.

Of course, John the Baptist had preached a "baptism of repentance for the forgiveness of sins." In fact, as we noted earlier, John's entire ministry revolved around Repentance. But now he was gone, and his remaining disciples must have felt like rather a lonely little group indeed.

When Paul came across this bunch of about a dozen men, he was obviously a little perplexed – and immediately began to ask them questions about where they had come from and what they believed. It seems clear that though he could see they were "disciples" and 'believers' of a kind, something was wrong – something was missing.

So how did they respond to what Paul had to tell them? Below is a Mini Bible Study where we look at exactly what happened. Quite an interesting account:

MINI BIBLE STUDY - ESSENTIAL

As usual, please look up each Scripture and write your answers to the questions below (or on another sheet if you wish)-

(a) Please READ Acts 19:1-6. Do you think there was much need to

preach Repentance to these people? Give reasons for your answer.

ANSWER - _____

_____

(b) What do you think prompted Paul to ask the question, "Did you receive the Holy Spirit when you believed?"

ANSWER - _____

_____

(c) Write out the now-familiar "pattern" of what happened to these people when they responded to the gospel preached by Paul.

ANSWER - _____

_____

(d) Do you think we can now say that this pattern is well established in Scripture?

ANSWER - _____

(e) How could Paul tell that they had been filled with the Holy Spirit?

ANSWER - _____

(f) Do you think that the "laying on of hands" was important?

ANSWER - _____

A PATTERN CONFIRMED

It almost goes without saying that once again there is nothing like the modern Sinner's Prayer in evidence in the above account. Need we say more?

However, in regard to the familiar pattern that we have been following throughout the Book of Acts, I don't know if we could get a more "textbook" confirmation than this one. The account is brief, detailed and to the point. And what do we see in evidence, once again?- (1) Repentance, (2) Faith, (3) Baptism, and (4) Receiving the Holy Spirit (through the laying on of hands). How could it get any clearer than that? Isn't it true that we are probably at the point now where we can start making some bold statements about what we have seen?

Firstly, it seems to me that we can now begin to talk about what a real "New Testament conversion" involves – and what it does not involve. And we can be bold about it because we have seen the same pattern repeating itself over and over again. Furthermore, I can tell you, having studied this subject for some years, that there is no account in the whole Book of Acts that goes against the pattern we have seen here. It is right there in black and white, time after time. And I don't believe anyone can deny it.

So where does this leave the people who are entrusting their salvation to a "little prayer" that they prayed in some meeting somewhere? Well, unless they follow through with full obedience to the real New Testament gospel, I believe they are left in a very precarious position indeed.

According to the Bible, a true New Testament Christian is someone who has (1) Repented, (2) Believed, (3) Been water-baptized, and (4) Been filled with the Holy Spirit. And in Scripture, all of this basically happened on the first day! This is "Day One" Christianity that we are talking about here!

We know that today there are all kinds of people living all kinds of lives who claim the name "Christian". But I am not too interested in what they "claim". I am interested in whether or not they have fulfilled what the Bible tells us we need to fulfill. I am interested in whether or not they have experienced true "Bible" conversion – in all its fullness. I don't want people with a 'half' salvation finding themselves in front of a Holy God on Judgment day. I want people to have the full New Testament conversion experience – and be living it.

Surely nothing less will do – and if we settle for less then we are short-changing all the people under our care. For this failure, will not many preachers find themselves off-side with a Holy God on that penultimate day when He judges the living and the dead?

I can't speak for you, but I know that personally I want to be found preaching a totally full gospel, a totally full New Testament Christianity, and a totally full conversion experience. And I cannot go along with any theory or doctrine that preaches anything less.

Chapter Eight

THE PATTERN OF JESUS
AND THE PATTERN OF ACTS

One thing that might be very valuable to do at this point is to go back to the life of Jesus Himself – and look at what happened at the very start of His ministry. Perhaps we can learn something important about the pattern we have seen in Acts from the life and words of Christ Himself.

We are told about the baptism of Jesus in three of the gospels – Matthew, Mark and Luke – and it is alluded to in John as well. Clearly it was a very important event in the life and ministry of Christ. In the Mini Bible Study below we take a closer look at what we can learn from His baptism.

MINI BIBLE STUDY - ESSENTIAL

As usual, please look up each Scripture and write your answers to the questions below-

(a) Please READ Matt 3:13-17. What was the reason that Jesus gave for why he needed to be baptized?

ANSWER - _____

(b) In verse 16, what is the "pattern" that we see for the first time? What happened when Jesus was baptized?

ANSWER - _____

(c) Do you think it was this "pattern" of John the Baptist and Jesus that basically became the "conversion" pattern that we see in Acts?

ANSWER - _____

CHRIST – OUR EXAMPLE

Isn't it interesting what Jesus said when he was questioned on his own need to be baptized? "Thus it is fitting for us to fulfill all righteousness" (Mt 3:15). What a significant answer in relation to baptism. "To fulfill all righteousness." A vital insight from Christ's own mouth.

And then when he actually got baptized, the Holy Spirit descended upon him in the form of a dove. Again, this has to be deeply significant in view of the pattern we have seen throughout Acts. Clearly the "conversion" pattern we have been noticing is simply modeled on the example of Christ himself.

In fact, couldn't it be said that John the Baptist's pattern of "a baptism of repentance for the forgiveness of sins" along with Jesus's pattern of the Holy Spirit descending after water-baptism – that these two things provided the foundation for every conversion seen in the New Testament? Of course this makes perfect sense when you think about it. Christ is supposed to be our example, after all. And if, for him, the whole thing began with "baptism in water and the Spirit," then obviously it should for us too.

BRIEF CONFIRMATIONS

To complete our look at the Acts of the Apostles, it may help us to briefly examine a couple of the less-detailed accounts of conversions found there to see what we can learn from them. One important point that we have mentioned – but not yet looked at in any depth – is the issue of how soon people got baptized in the Bible. Did they have to wait six weeks or six months - or was it always immediate? The Mini Bible Study below seeks to answer this question – though in many ways it confirms what we have already seen. However, it is still important to look at.

The conversions of the Jailer and the Ethiopian Eunuch are only briefly recounted in the Book of Acts. But we can still learn quite a lot from them – even though some of the detail is lacking. Please complete the Mini Bible Study below which looks at these two conversions:

MINI BIBLE STUDY - ESSENTIAL

As always, please look up each Scripture and write your answers to the questions below (or on another sheet if you wish)-

(a) Please READ Acts 16:25-33. At roughly what time of day were the Jailer and his family baptized?

ANSWER - _____

(b) Does the above passage give the impression that baptism is very important? In what way?

ANSWER - _____

(c) Please READ Acts 8:35-38. Do you think Philip spoke about baptism when he was preaching the gospel to the Eunuch? How can you tell?

ANSWER - _____

_____

(d) How soon was the Eunuch baptized?

ANSWER - _____

(e) Was there any kind of "special ceremony" required – or "witnesses" – or special robes needed?

ANSWER - _____

(f) Based on these passages, and all that we have seen, how soon do you think we should baptize people?

ANSWER – _____

IMPORTANT AND IMMEDIATE

Isn't it interesting in the above passages how quickly these people were taken and baptized? Even in the middle of the night! There was seemingly no delay at all. And of course, this lines up with everything else that we have seen in Acts. The people seemed to be water-baptized without delay in every account that we have looked at. Of course, this points to the fact that the apostles considered baptism to be far more vital than most of us do today. There was clearly an importance to baptism back then that we seem to have utterly lost. (More on this in the next chapter).

Another thing that is notable in the above accounts is that they clearly seemed to be preaching about baptism as part of the gospel. We see this most blatantly with the Ethiopian Eunuch. Philip is simply preaching the gospel to him, when suddenly he exclaims, "Here is water. What is stopping me from getting baptized?" So there can be little question that baptism was part of the gospel that Philip preached to him. Do any dare preach this way today?

THE PATTERN IS UNDENIABLE

With these last two brief accounts, we have now looked at basically EVERY conversion that is detailed in the entire book of Acts. From beginning to end, we have searched out every detailed description we can find. And the fact is, from all we can see, there is simply no "Ask Jesus into your heart", no "Repeat this little prayer", no "Give your heart to the Lord" in the entire book.

Why is this so important? As we noted earlier, the Book of Acts is quite simply the only history we have of the early years of the church. If someone comes up with a conversion method today that is not found in this book, then how can it be scriptural? If we don't see the apostles doing it, then why should we accept it? And worse still, if it is actually an unbiblical "replacement" for what the apostles did and preached, then shouldn't we be fighting against it with all our might?

There is nothing more important than people's salvation. They should be able to at least rely on us to tell them the truth about this one thing. When they ask, "Men and brothers, what shall we do?" then we ought to have the correct answer. This is one of the major reasons why the church even exists – to tell the world how to be forgiven and saved. So how can it be that we have managed to lose our grip on even this most basic truth?

Don't you find it disturbing that when people ask us, "What shall we do?" today, that our answer is utterly different from the apostles? Don't you find it alarming that our answer almost couldn't be more different if it tried? "Just repeat this little prayer – asking Jesus into your heart." What kind of sub-scriptural half-job is that? What kind of non-salvation? What kind of cheap placebo? What kind of shallow plastic imitation of the real thing?

Isn't this the worst form of falsehood that it is possible to imagine? To go around the whole world falsely assuring people that they are "saved" when the Bible says otherwise. It just doesn't bear thinking about – the damage we have been doing – does it? We have gone right around the globe preaching the wrong thing. And it is to do with people's SALVATION – the most important subject of all.

I don't know about you, but after I myself was confronted with this truth many years ago, I determined in my heart that I was going to preach the apostolic pattern from then on – and nothing less. When people wanted to know, "What shall we do?" then I was going to tell them what Peter told the people on the Day of Pentecost – "REPENT, and be BAPTIZED every one of you in the name of Jesus Christ for the remission of sins, and you shall receive the gift of the HOLY SPIRIT" (Acts 2:38). I still cannot come up with any answer that is better than this for representing what the apostles preached throughout the Book of Acts. To me, it is clearly the biblical pattern – confirmed over and over again. And I hope for anyone reading this, that if someone comes to you with the same question, then you too would now seek to give the exact same answer. To me, it really has to be the Bible way or no way at all. Amen?

In coming chapters we are going to see that it is not just the Book of Acts, but actually the entire New Testament that preaches the same thing. We have had the truth hidden from our eyes for too long. It is time to lift the veil on these most obvious truths – and get the church preaching what the apostles always preached. So our journey of discovery is not over yet. And our next port of call is to take a much closer look at what baptism truly means.

CHAPTER NINE

THE TRUE MEANING OF BAPTISM

One of the key questions that we will be seeking to answer from now on is this:- Does the rest of the New Testament support what we have just seen in Acts? Is the same pattern preached throughout?

We have already looked at the first two "foundations" – Repentance and Faith – earlier in this book. Now it is time to look at baptism. What exactly does the Bible have to say about it? Is it merely some kind of "outward symbol" – or is it deeper than that? What is the true meaning of baptism, according to Scripture? And just how "essential" is it?

Most evangelical groups around the world describe water baptism as merely an "outward symbol of an inner change." Thus baptism is stripped of much of its significance and power in Christian thinking – and a lower priority tends to be put on it. For a symbol is never as important as the "real thing," is it? Thus we find evangelicals who have not even been baptized after several years of believing the gospel – or who are waiting to go through a six-month "baptismal class," etc. The whole idea that baptism is merely some kind of 'symbol' leads to a whole raft of subtle "downgrades" that are both unfortunate and unscriptural.

So what does the Bible actually teach about water baptism? Is it mostly just an outward symbol - or is there something powerful happening SPIRITUALLY when someone is baptized? The Mini Bible Study below seeks to answer these vital questions. Please complete it if at all possible.

MINI BIBLE STUDY - ESSENTIAL

As always, please look up each Scripture and write your answers to the questions below-

(a) Please READ Rom 6:3-8. According to this passage, what happens to our "old life" through baptism?

ANSWER - _____

(b) According to verses 3 and 4, by what means do we become "buried" into the death of Christ?

ANSWER - _____

(c) Going by this passage in Romans 6, how important does baptism appear to be?

ANSWER - _____

(d) Please READ Col 2:11-12. According to this passage, what is happening inside of us when we are baptized?

ANSWER - _____

(e) Please describe what the term "circumcision of the heart" means to you-

ANSWER - _____

BURIAL OF THE OLD LIFE

It is important to note that there is not one Scripture in the entire New Testament that describes baptism as merely "symbolic" – or simply a ritual that we need to go through. As we have seen in the two passages above, the Bible describes baptism as being a 'circumcision of the heart', a "cutting off", a "burial" into the death of Christ. What could be more important than something like that?

Picture a prison inmate – convicted of the ghastly crimes of rape or murder. Imagine if you said to this man, "Sir, what would you give to have your entire past cut-off and got rid of – your old life buried and put to death with all its evil deeds? What would you give to have the old 'you' cut off and washed away?" This man would be overjoyed at such a thing. It is his old rotten 'self' and its sinful deeds that put him in jail in the first place. How glad he would be to be separated from it all!

This is exactly what baptism does, according to Scripture. It kills and buries our old self. It is a "cutting off" of the flesh, a 'circumcision' of the heart, a death and burial of our old life. It unites us with Christ in death, so that we can be raised up into a new life in Him. This is precisely what Romans 6 says about it.

I am convinced that from God's point of view – in the 'spirit' realm – there is a lot happening when someone is baptized. It is tempting for man simply to look on the 'outward appearance' and say, "Oh, it is just someone being dipped in the water." But that is not God's point of view at all. It is clear that in the spirit realm there is much more going on. And Scripture certainly bears this out. No wonder the apostles always baptized people right away! Even in the middle of the night! Now we know the reason. Baptism is clearly meant to be a very powerful event indeed.

Some leaders say that it is self-defeating to baptize people right away, because they are "not ready" – and it is important to take them through "preparation classes" so that they become committed to the Christian life before baptism. In a lot of cases, what these leaders are trying to do is make up for is a lack of Repentance and also the lack of a piercing, life-changing gospel. They need to spend all this time "preparing" people because of the inadequate gospel that has been preached to them. Instead, what they should be doing is preaching a bold, convicting, heart-piercing message in the first place - and then their converts would "stick". If their gospel was anointed and powerful (as it should be) then there would be no need for lengthy "preparation classes" before baptism. (We discuss how to preach this way in a later chapter). Under a biblical gospel, people should be ready right away.

I cannot go along with any method or program that takes us away from the biblical pattern. If it was good enough for the apostles and evangelists in Acts, then it is good enough for us. Like the Bible, we need to see people repenting and getting baptized right away. No excuses!

I usually find it only takes two minutes to explain to people what baptism is all about. I read from Romans 6 and tell them that baptism is the "death and burial" of their old life – a 'cutting off' of the old man – a "death to self". Within a couple of minutes I find that they understand – and they're ready to go. And quite often we see people filled with the Holy Spirit – either when they are baptized or soon after. This is exactly what is supposed to happen.

There is no excuse not to do things the Bible way. The whole reason the church is in such a mess today is because we have ignored the ways of Scripture and of the early church. It is high time that we get back to Book of Acts Christianity – just as it was founded by Jesus and the apostles. It has to be the Bible way or nothing. And baptism is just one of the many ways that we've been falling short.

SPRINKLING & INFANT BAPTISM

For centuries there have been more "traditional" churches that have used 'sprinkling' or making the "sign of the cross" on someone's forehead to baptize them. The major problem with this is that the Greek word used for baptism in the Bible is "baptizo" - which means to "dip or immerse". Every time they tell us in Scripture that someone got baptized, in the original Greek it is saying that they got "dipped or immersed" in the water. And virtually everyone who studies the original Bible languages today admits that this was the case.

After all, as we have seen, baptism is described in the Bible as a "burial". Therefore, just like a real burial where a person is buried right under the earth, surely it follows that baptism has to be by "full immersion" under the water. Doesn't this make perfect sense?

History shows that the tradition of "sprinkling" only came about after centuries of decline in the church – as she slowly descended into the Dark Ages. As far as we can tell by studying the writings of the "church fathers" of the second and third centuries, the practice of 'sprinkling' did not become common until a couple of hundred years after the apostles. Up until then it was almost always baptism by "full immersion" – just like in the early church. But slowly as the centuries went by, the church lost her grip on baptism, just as she had begun to lose her grip on so much else.

So what about infant baptism? Obviously, the main objection to baptizing little babies is that they cannot yet "believe" the gospel. The Bible clearly states that, "He who believes and is baptized will be saved" (Mark 16:16a). So it is vital to believe first before baptism. And in fact we see this in the "foundations" of Hebrews 6:1-2 as well. In that passage, Repentance and Faith both come before baptism – and of course this makes perfect sense. Someone must be old enough to understand and believe the gospel before they can become a true Christian.

Some traditionalists try to make a case for infant baptism by pointing out that several times the Scriptures speak of entire "households" coming to the Lord. However, what they fail to mention is that we are not told that there were any infants in any of those households. And if there were tiny children present, we are certainly not told that they were baptized.

It is very clear in Scripture that baptism is for believers – not babies. And again, if we read the "church fathers" we can see that infant baptism only become popular several centuries after the apostles – as the church descended more and more into full-blown apostasy.

Believer's baptism by full immersion was the norm in Bible days, and it ought to be the norm for us as well.

WHO CAN BAPTIZE?

Many Christians think that only elders and pastors are allowed to baptize. But there is no such restriction in Scripture. In fact, as we saw in an earlier chapter, Saul (who later became the apostle Paul) was baptized by a man who was simply described as "a certain disciple at Damascus named Ananias." We are not told that he was an elder or anyone amazingly special. All we know is that he was a true, Spirit-filled Christian. He was simply God's "man on the spot". In fact, nowhere in the New Testament do we find restrictions laid down as to who may baptize and who may not.

One of the things I love to do when I am ministering to Christian Youth is to release them to be baptizers. All I have to do to is teach them from Scripture that there is nothing stopping them from baptizing others. In fact, Jesus sent us all out baptizing! He said, "Go therefore and make disciples of all the nations, baptizing them in the name of the Father and of the Son and of the Holy Spirit" (Matt 28:19). So we are actually commanded by Jesus to go and baptize people!

When the young people are released to do this, I often hear stories afterwards that warm my heart. Perhaps some of them will have baptized a homeless man in the river, or preached the gospel to their unsaved friends and baptized them – praying for them to be filled with the Holy Spirit while they are at it - or casting out demons, etc. What I find is that when people start doing "New Testament" things they find that life goes up a gear – and they often find themselves living out little bits of the New Testament all over the place!

The reason a lot of us never experience true New Testament Christianity is because we don't do things the New Testament way. If we want to experience the purity and power of the early church then we are going to have to start preaching the same gospel and doing the same things that they did. Suddenly we may find ourselves living on a spiritual plane that we never expected – simply by doing New Testament things the New Testament way. I have seen this happen again and again. And baptizing is a great place to start. Go and try it!

BAPTIZING IN THE NAME OF THE LORD

During our exploration of the Book of Acts, you may have noticed something interesting about the way people were baptized. We are often told that they were baptized "in the name of Jesus Christ" or "in the name of the Lord". And yet, as we have just seen, when Jesus sent His followers out He commanded them to baptize people "in the name of the Father and of the Son and of the Holy Spirit" (Mt 28:19). So why is there this difference? Why the name of Jesus Christ on one hand, and "Father, Son and Holy Spirit" on the other?

To be honest, we do not know why. But I think it is something we should take note of. If they felt it was important in Acts to speak the name of Jesus Christ over people as they were baptized, then probably we should do it too. I am not legalistic about the need for this, but personally these days I baptize people "in the name of the Father and the Son and the Holy Spirit - in the name of JESUS CHRIST." (-To make sure all the bases are covered!!)

This may not be a major point, but it certainly is worth being aware of.

CHAPTER TEN

COMMON OBJECTIONS

There are a number of objections that people often raise when they hear the kind of teaching that we are bringing forth in this book. Often they are trying to defend the idea that all we need to do is "pray a little prayer" to become a true 'Bible Christian'. They do not want to admit that the scriptural pattern is (1) Repentance, (2) Faith, (3) Baptism, and (4) Receiving the Holy Spirit. Below are some of the main objections that people often raise – and our response:

One of the most common verses that is used to support the idea of 'Asking Jesus into your heart' is Rev 3:20 – "Behold I stand at the door and knock..." Of course this sounds quite convincing until you actually look up the passage and discover how out-of-context it is. The whole of this Revelation 3 passage is not aimed at non-Christians at all – but rather the lukewarm church! It is not about unbelievers inviting Jesus into their heart, but rather lukewarm Christians inviting Jesus back in to be truly Lord of His church! Take a look, in the Bible Study below:-

BRIEF BIBLE STUDY

(a) Please READ Rev 3:14-22. Is this entire passage written to Christians or non-Christians?

ANSWER - _____

(b) Is it about the state of unbelievers' hearts toward God, or rather about the state of the Laodicean church?

ANSWER - _____

(c) Since it is written to the church, do you think it may be out-of-context to apply such a passage to non-Christians, and use it to support the idea of "Asking Jesus into your heart"?

ANSWER - _____

(2) Another very common objection that people raise is the "Thief on the cross". They say that since Jesus promised the Thief a place with Him in paradise – even though he seemingly repented only at the last minute – then this is proof for the Sinner's Prayer approach.

OUR ANSWER: There is no doubt that this is a good example of "death-bed" repentance – which is definitely something we believe in. In other words, when people are literally at death's door, we certainly believe that they can still repent and make their peace with God – even at the last possible minute. But does this mean that the Thief should be taken as an example of "normal" conversion? Is this an example that everyone should follow?

One very important thing that should be noted is that this event took place BEFORE the New Covenant truly began – before Jesus was resurrected and before the Spirit was given at Pentecost. Therefore, how can it be a good example for us to follow if we want to experience a full New Testament conversion? Was the Thief even "born-again" as such, since the New Covenant had not even truly begun yet, or did he just get a last-minute reprieve? Was this a normal New Testament conversion in any sense?

Our own conclusion is – "No." This was not a normal NT conversion, and not an example that we should follow in order to have a full and true conversion experience under the New Covenant. But it is certainly a good example of "death-bed repentance".

(3) Another objection which people often raise is what they call the 'Romans Road' of conversion found in Romans 10. This is usually quoted as a kind-of "formula" for becoming a Christian – and is the main Scriptural passage used in support of the Sinner's Prayer.

In the Mini Bible Study below we take a look at this passage and whether or not it is, in fact, evidence for "Asking Jesus into your heart."

MINI BIBLE STUDY - ESSENTIAL

As always, please look up each Scripture and write your answers to the questions below (or on another sheet if you wish)-

(a) Please READ Rom 10:9-13. Perhaps the first question we should ask is:- Is this passage meant to be an actual 'formula' for salvation? Is that the actual purpose of it? Please give your opinion.

ANSWER - _____

(b) This is a wonderful passage about FAITH - a very important topic. But who is it written to - believers or unbelievers? Who is the book of Romans aimed at?

ANSWER - _____

(c) Do you believe that Rom 10 might perhaps be written differently if it really was a "salvation formula" being written to unbelievers?

ANSWER - _____

(d) When we look at the overwhelming evidence on the side of "Repentance, Baptism & Receiving the Spirit" - and we look at the fact that we cannot find anyone in the whole Book of Acts simply "praying a little prayer" for salvation - shouldn't we go with the overwhelming Bible way? In other words, does the "weight" of Scripture matter? Isn't this what we should always do in these situations - go with what the overwhelming "weight" of Scripture tells us? Please give your opinion.

ANSWER - _____

(e) Rom 10:13 says that "Whoever calls on the name of the Lord shall be saved". But here is an important question:- When did Paul himself actually 'call on the name of the Lord'? When did this moment occur for him? Please READ Acts 22:16 once again and write below the actual words that Ananias spoke to him:

ANSWER - _____

_____

(f) As the above passage shows, it was actually in BAPTISM that Paul truly "called on the name of the Lord." Do you believe that this may have been a common application of this Scripture back then? In other words, is it possible that this 'calling on the name of the Lord' often took place for the first time in baptism?

ANSWER - _____

CONCLUSIONS ON ROMANS 10

There is no question that the above passage in Romans is the best argument that modern preachers have for "Giving your heart to the Lord" or praying a Sinner's Prayer.

However, at the end of the day I do not find Rom 10 to be conclusive proof against the conversion pattern that we found in Acts - or strong enough backing for the idea of a "little prayer". To me, it does not make sense to take that meaning from it when the whole rest of the New Testament teaches otherwise. I have to go with the "weight" of Scripture – and the overwhelming pattern of the apostles.

This is a general principle that we should always apply when one Scripture seems to contradict all the others on any subject. We should always go with the "weight" of Scripture. In other words, we should go with what the overwhelming preponderance of verses are telling us. And to me, these do not support the idea of a 'little prayer' being adequate at all.

And in regard to "calling on the name of the Lord," it is clear that Paul actually did this himself during BAPTISM. I used to attend a fellowship that practiced a very similar thing. They would use Romans 10 simply as a "baptismal confession" for anyone who was getting baptized.

(4) Another common question that people often ask is, "What about the old Revivalists and Reformers from past centuries? The Christianity of their time did not involve Baptism by Immersion or being filled with the Holy Spirit. What about these heroes of old?"

OUR ANSWER: I actually believe that God has slowly been restoring His truths to the church bit by bit over the centuries, since the Great Reformation. All that had been lost is slowly returning. If you look at history you will see that it started with the preaching of "Justification by Faith" in the 1500s, then the "New Birth" and Sanctification in the 1700s, then Baptism by Immersion, then healing, then Baptism of the Spirit with 'tongues', etc, until today we have the opportunity to fully enter into virtually everything that the early church entered into - and powerful Spirit-filled Revivals are happening around the globe.

The church has come full circle in many ways, but still I feel we need one last Great Reformation to fully restore all that was lost. It has taken a very long time for the church to emerge out of the Dark Ages, and there have been many "heroes" along the way. To me, men like Luther, Wesley, Whitefield, Finney, etc, are a great inspiration - and I write about them and preach about them all the time. But yes - they lived in an era when Christianity seemingly had less 'restored' than she does today. Thus I believe all the people of those times will be judged according to the light that they walked in. It is as simple as that. I do not condemn them at all - in fact I admire many of those old preachers and learn as much from them as I can.

(5) Another question that people often ask is - "Do you believe in Baptismal Regeneration?"

OUR ANSWER: No! We certainly do NOT believe in Baptismal Regeneration - which is basically an old Catholic doctrine. All we are saying is simply that the Bible way of becoming converted is through Repentance, Faith, Baptism and Receiving the Holy Spirit. We believe in ALL these elements. We certainly do not believe that people can be regenerated just by being plunged under the water.

I often find that people who accuse us of "Baptismal Regeneration" are trying to distract people away from the real issues – trying to "label" us and what we are saying before people get a chance to check it out for themselves. Sadly they sometimes succeed in this. However, we regard what we are preaching as completely orthodox Christian teaching – both biblically and historically. We believe it is the concept of "repeating a little prayer to ask Jesus into your heart" that is actually heretical – and carries very little support – either scripturally or from church history. The Sinner's Prayer concept has not even been around for very long. It was seemingly invented over the last 70 years or so as a "convenient" method for use in mass-evangelism, etc. It actually has far less historical and biblical validity than the truths we have been presenting in this book.

(6) Another question that people often ask is - "Couldn't this be seen as a kind-of Salvation by works?"

OUR ANSWER: Absolutely not! Where are the "works"? Is Faith a work? Is Repentance a 'work'? Is water-baptism a work? (It is quick, it happens only once, and the person does not even do it to themselves - so how can they be "working"?) Is receiving the Holy Spirit a work? In my opinion, none of these things are remotely like works at all. Where is the "working" going on?

If we perhaps think of the typical conversion that we have seen in the Book of Acts, we see what nonsense this truly is. Think of the Ephesians, for instance. They have already repented under John the Baptist's ministry. (And even repentance is only by the grace of God working in the heart of man). On the day they meet Paul they are baptized by him in water and when he lays hands upon them they receive the Holy Spirit very powerfully. Does this whole thing sound like "works" to you? Does it smack of "working" for your salvation? No – it comes across as God's grace from beginning to end – a God given doorway that we enter by His divine enabling – a moment of time that changes one's life forever. The whole process does not have 'works' written over it – but rather "grace". And it only takes a moment. It is simply an "entry-point" – not a lifestyle of "working" for your salvation.

CONCLUDING COMMENTS

The above objections are by far the most common ones that people raise when they come across the teachings that we present in this book. In my view, they are simply not adequate to overturn the very obvious pattern of conversion that we find in the Book of Acts or in the "foundations" of Hebrews 6. And as we shall see in coming chapters, this pattern is also confirmed again and again right through the rest of the New Testament. I simply cannot go along with any pattern that is not the pattern of the apostles or of Jesus Himself. I hope that this chapter has adequately dealt with the objections that people raise, so we can move on to the insights that lie ahead.

CHAPTER ELEVEN

MY OWN EXPERIENCE

When I was a young man of seventeen I attended a local Baptist church in the area where my parents lived. This was not a "Charismatic" Baptist or anything, but it did have quite a lively Youth Group and a number of young people who were unusually committed to God. However, for the most part I was not there for particularly spiritual reasons, but rather for the social contacts, to meet girls, and because my parents made me go – as long as I remained under their roof. But I could often be found skipping Youth Group to play Arcade games down the street.

This was a particularly dangerous moment in my spiritual life, because I had now left school and started work. I was not a truly committed Christian and a wider adult world with its varied temptations sparkled and glinted all around. But God had things well in hand.

I had been brought up all my life in the church – of various evangelical denominations. When I was very young we were with the Open Brethren and the Baptists. Then we had a stint with the Assemblies of God. And now we were back with the Baptists again.

My father had been a Baptist preacher before I was born, but was now teaching school instead. He was a Spirit-filled praying man who always brought us up with strong Christian values. But he was also a real disciplinarian and I was filled with resentment towards him. In fact, it was more than just resentment. My life was filled with hate and bitterness, and because of this I suffered from terrible depression. Almost every day I desperately wanted to end my life. It went on like this for years. A life filled with misery, hatred, suicidal thoughts and despair.

I lost all confidence and became bullied at school – which only made things worse. My life was in turmoil. I don't know if you can imagine what it's like being filled with a longing to end your life every day. Trudging on for month after month, year after year, wanting only to die. For four long years, between the ages of 13 and 17, that's what it was like for me almost every day.

A POWERLESS BELIEF

For years I tried saying the "Sinner's Prayer," but seemingly to no avail. I had initially made some kind of commitment to Christ – and apparently meant it – way back when I was just five years old. I was even baptized a couple of years later – and I believe I truly understood what I was doing. But there was no "power" at all to my faith. No power over sin, no power over the world, no power to walk it out. As I got into my teen years I could tell I was not a true Christian inside. I went to church every week but it was all hollow. And so I would find myself alone at night in my room, filled with utter despair, forlornly repeating the words of the "Sinner's Prayer" just as I'd done a hundred times before - with no result.

I had no backbone to my belief. When other kids smoked, I smoked just to try and fit in. When they swore, I swore. I don't know who I was trying to kid. Nobody was the least bit impressed – least of all me. I was a misfit, an outcast, a walking disaster area.

And then it happened.

We had moved house after I finished High School and I was now attending the local Baptist Youth Group that I mentioned earlier. Some of my Youth Group friends were starting to get very serious about seeking God. A couple of them told me about an experience they'd had in which a man "laid hands" on them and they were filled with the Holy Spirit and spoke in 'tongues'. I was a little freaked out by this, as I had come across "tongues" when my family attended the

Pentecostal church and I didn't like it much. In fact, it frightened me. But I couldn't ignore the changes I noticed in my friends. There was a kind-of holy "presence" around them now that I couldn't deny. They were definitely different, and it started to affect me.

All through my teenage years, whenever there was an altar-call to "completely surrender" myself to God, I had always resisted. Sometimes I even gripped onto my chair to stop myself going forward. I don't know why I was so reluctant to truly surrender all. My life was a literal hellhole. I spent half my days longing to die. Why I would not want to surrender a life like that, I have no idea. But perhaps even though it was a hellhole, it was "my" hellhole. I guess that was it. I still wanted to be in charge.

But hanging around my newly Spirit-filled friends was having quite an effect on me. And I knew where it was heading. It was heading toward "total surrender".

I remember the occasion very well. I remember sitting in my mother's car and literally surrendering every part of my life – all that I was and all that I would ever be – to God. And I remember literally shaking as His presence came over me powerfully at that moment. And I knew the next thing that had to happen was for me to get filled with the Holy Spirit.

And so, I went to the same man that my friends had been to. He was a sound, Bible-believing man. I asked him to "lay hands" and pray for me. And instantly I was literally filled to overflowing with the love, the power and the presence of a holy God. As simple as that. And the terrible cloud of hatred and depression that had been over me all those years lifted off and dissipated in a moment. I didn't even think about it. I only realized later that it was gone. All I knew was that I had a smile on my face a mile wide. And the very next day I spoke in "tongues" for the first time.

TONGUES AND TRANSFORMATION

So what exactly is 'tongues'? As we see in Scripture, it is simply a new language that God gives us to worship and pray to Him with. (More on this in the next chapter). It is the "holy utterance" of God. And today I find when I'm preaching that the more I pray in tongues before I preach the word, the more powerful, convicting and anointed it will be. Tongues is an awesome prayer-weapon that God gives us – for free!

So what was the result in my life of this whole experience? Utter transformation! I was literally a new person. The old Andrew was gone. No longer was I a timid, compromising "hollow" believer. I was literally on fire for God. I suddenly found I had a tremendous relationship and close communion with Him.

The love and power of God had filled my life. And His holiness also. The baptism of the "HOLY" Spirit is a baptism of holiness. And I definitely experienced this – Christ's power and victory over sin. And the change was permanent. No going back. His Spirit has been with me ever since. I was seventeen years old and my life had been utterly and permanently transformed.

It should be no surprise to anyone that I regard this as the moment that I became truly converted – in the full Bible sense. I know for a fact that I did not have it in me to live as a true Christian before this. I could never say with Paul, "It is no longer I that live, but Christ that lives in me." That life-transforming faith and love that the New Testament speaks of again and again was simply not found in me. Not until that moment. And then everything changed in an instant. I was filled with faith, filled with boldness, filled with the love of Christ and a peace that "passes all understanding."

I regard my conversion as truly biblical – in the sense that it seems very similar to what we see in Acts. But isn't it a tragedy that a young man on the point of suicide spent all those years praying a "little prayer" that seemingly had no effect at all? I wonder how many thousands of people around the world are in the same tragic situation? Desperately wanting to know and be transformed by God, and yet no truly transforming gospel is ever preached to them. I believe such a tragedy is being played out on a vast scale.

I cannot believe in any conversion experience that is below that of the Bible. I cannot preach any conversion that is not that of the apostles. I am convinced that one of the huge reasons why the church is in the lukewarm state it is in today is because of the gospel we preach (or fail to preach). And we had better get back to the Bible fast, because an entire generation – and an entire world - is at stake. This cannot be something that God will "wink at" forever.

Where are the bold preachers today who will lay their life and reputation on the line, and stand up and declare the truth? Where are the men and women of God who love the people and the truth more than life itself – who will not be silent when a lost generation is perishing for lack of knowledge? Where are those who will "cry aloud and spare not" in this present age? God is waiting for bold preachers of righteousness to arise. And until they do there is surely little hope for our lukewarm church or our sin-soaked world. God awaits His "mighty men of valor," His reformers and revivalists, His pioneers and prophets. Tell me, friend, could this be you?

CHAPTER TWELVE

BAPTISM IN THE HOLY SPIRIT

It was John the Baptist who declared, "I indeed baptized you with water, but He will baptize you with the Holy Spirit" (Mk 1:8). Isn't that a significant statement, considering all that we have seen? Jesus is the great Baptizer – not merely with water – but with the very Holy Spirit of God.

Just before being taken up to heaven, Jesus commanded His disciples not to leave Jerusalem, but to wait for the "promise of the Father." And then He repeated virtually the same statement that John the Baptist had made: "John truly baptized with water, but you shall be baptized with the Holy Spirit not many days from now" (Acts 1:5).

And so the disciples waited in Jerusalem – gathered in the Upper Room for ten days – praying and waiting for the enduement from "on high" that Jesus had promised. And on the Day of Pentecost it came. The sound of a "mighty, rushing wind." Tongues of fire that appeared upon each of their heads. And suddenly, "They were all filled with the Holy Spirit and began to speak with other tongues, as the Spirit gave them utterance" (Acts 2:4).

So what is the purpose of this Holy Spirit baptism? Below is an important little Bible Study that shows what the Holy Spirit does in our lives. Please complete it if at all possible:

MINI BIBLE STUDY - ESSENTIAL

As always, please look up each Scripture and write your answers to the questions below-

(a) Please READ John 16:13-14. According to verse 13, what will the Holy Spirit guide them into – and also tell them?

ANSWER - _____

_____

(b) According to verse 14, who will the Holy Spirit glorify?

ANSWER - _____

(c) Please READ Acts 1:8. What will they receive when the Holy Spirit comes upon them?

ANSWER - _____

(d) And what will this experience turn them into?

ANSWER - _____

(e) Please READ Rom 5:5. According to this Scripture, how exactly is the love of God poured out in our hearts?

ANSWER - _____

(f) Please READ Gal 5:22-23 and write out the "fruit" of the Holy Spirit:

ANSWER - _____

_____

(g) Please READ Rom 8:13-14. According to verse 13, how do we "put to death" the deeds of the body?

ANSWER - _____

(h) According to verse 14, who is a son of God?

ANSWER - _____

GIFTS OF THE SPIRIT AND LAYING ON OF HANDS

As we have seen above, the Holy Spirit is incredibly important in our lives for many reasons. He brings to mind the things Christ has taught, leads us into all truth, shows us things to come and glorifies Jesus. He also gives us power to be witnesses for Christ, fills our heart with the love of God, and allows us to defeat the flesh by walking in the Spirit. We could go on and on, looking at the wonderful results of having the Holy Spirit filling our life. Clearly this is essential to every aspect of "normal" Christianity presented in the Bible. It is utterly unimaginable having any kind of real Christianity without the Holy Spirit.

We are also told that there are nine "gifts" that the Holy Spirit gives out as well. These are:- (1) Word of wisdom, (2) Word of knowledge, (3) Faith, (4) Gifts of healing, (5) Miracles, (6) Prophecy, (7) Discerning of spirits, (8) Different kinds of tongues, and (9) Interpretation of tongues.

So the Holy Spirit is very powerful and "supernatural" in His operation in our lives. And we need to let this power and presence of God flow through us to the greatest possible degree. Only then can we hope to reach this generation the same way that Jesus and the apostles reached theirs. We have to let the Holy Spirit flow!

As we saw at the start of this book, one of the six 'foundations' found in Hebrews 6:1-2 is "the laying on of hands." And three times we saw in Acts that people actually received the Holy Spirit through having hands laid upon them. I myself had exactly this same experience. And there is no question that we must make it a practice to "lay hands" on people and pray for them to receive God's Spirit today. This is totally scriptural - and to have powerless "believers" around who have not yet received the Holy Spirit just doesn't bear thinking about.

RECEIVED OR "BAPTIZED WITH" – THE SAME THING?

There are a number of groups today who try to make a distinction between "receiving" the Holy Spirit and being 'baptized' or "filled" with the Holy Spirit. As we saw in Acts, such a distinction simply does not apply. The apostles used all these terms interchangeably. But this scares a lot of people – because they are fully aware that many people are not getting baptized with the Holy Spirit. And they want to make this "OK". They want to make it OK to have a 'lesser' Christianity. They want to make it OK to have no power and no deep transforming experience with God. They want to make it OK just to "pray a little prayer."

These are the people who almost got me killed as a teenager. They think a powerless Christianity is "fine". I want to say to these people as clearly as I can, that a powerless Christianity is no Christianity at all. And I wonder how many others there are whose lives are being ruined by such "half-measures" and a 'half-gospel'.

As we saw earlier, the best place to see these terms being used interchangeably - and applied to exactly the same experience - is in Acts chapters 10 and 11. In Acts 10:45-47 we see the terms "poured out on" and 'received the Spirit' together. Then in Acts 11:15-18 we see the terms 'fell upon' and "baptized with the Spirit" being applied to the exact same event – and also to the apostles' experience at Pentecost. This, of course, means that being "filled" and 'receiving' and being "baptized" in the Holy Spirit are all exactly the same thing.

And as we have seen, this experience is not merely some "optional extra". It is absolutely essential to the Christian life. And it must be preached as such.

TONGUES IN THE BIBLE

The classic Pentecostal position regarding "tongues" is that generally this is the 'initial evidence' of getting filled with the Holy Spirit. In other words, Pentecostals see tongues as a kind of "first outward sign" of Holy Spirit baptism. As Frank Bartleman of the Azusa Street Revival wrote: "All who received this 'baptism' spoke in 'tongues.'" (pg 62). This is essentially what I have come to believe also.

Let us take a closer look at this subject, starting with the Bible Study below. Again, this Study is very important, so please complete it if at all possible:

MINI BIBLE STUDY - ESSENTIAL

As always, please look up each Scripture and write your answers to the questions below (or on another sheet if you wish)-

Firstly, please WRITE OUT each of the following verses-

(a) Mark 16:17.

ANSWER - _____

_____

(b) Acts 2:4.

ANSWER - _____

_____

(c) Acts 10:45-46.

ANSWER - _____

_____

_____

(d) Acts 19:6.

ANSWER - _____

_____

(e) Acts 8:17-18.

ANSWER - _____

_____

_____

(f) 1 Cor 14:18.

ANSWER - _____

A BAPTISM OF HOLINESS

Of course, tongues are not the "be-all and end-all" of baptism in the Holy Spirit. They are simply an 'initial evidence' that we see in Scripture and also modern times when someone receives this infilling. It is very important not to get so hung-up on "tongues" that we forget the big picture of what this baptism of the Spirit is really all about. Our emphasis needs to be on the fact that it is a baptism of holiness, power, love and victory over sin - which are the most important things that we expect to see in a person's life after this experience. But I believe that tongues should be regarded as an important "initial evidence" - and vital for ongoing prayer also. Paul said, "I speak in tongues more than you all," so he obviously prayed in tongues a lot. Shouldn't we do likewise? As mentioned earlier, I myself find that the more I pray in tongues before I preach, the more anointed, effective and convicting my preaching seems to become.

OBJECTIONS TO 'TONGUES'

There are several objections that people often bring up. Some simply believe that the gifts of the Spirit are not for today at all. I must admit that this argument has never made much sense to me, and I certainly do not have time to go into it here. But the objection that we find most common is that many believe tongues is only for "some" Christians – certainly not 'all' as the Pentecostals believe.

And this is a very understandable misgiving that people have.

However, it is my belief that God desires ALL His children to have such a 'prayer-language'. The passage that seems to confuse people most is found in 1 Corinthians 12:29-30. Because this passage asks "Are all apostles, are all prophets... Do all speak in tongues?" (to which the obvious answer is "No"), people are left thinking that tongues is only for 'some'. But what they fail to notice is that this whole passage is speaking about "ministry gifts" in the church. The entire paragraph is listing 'ministry-offices' that some are called to. And one of these is to "speak out publicly" in tongues during a church meeting - which must always have interpretation. Only certain people are called to do this. That is the point Paul is making. They have a special calling and anointing to use tongues as a public ministry - which is not for everyone. But certainly he is not talking about the private "prayer language" that we believe Scripture shows is available to every believer.

My wife Jacqui is a good example of someone with this special gift and calling. Ever since the day that she was first filled with the Holy Spirit years ago, she has spoken out many times publicly in 'tongues' in Christian meetings. This must always be followed by an 'interpretation'. She also uses tongues quietly for private prayer – which is quite a different thing. Personally I have never felt called to speak out in tongues the way she does, but I use my private "prayer language" all the time. I simply do not feel that I am called or anointed to do what she does publicly in meetings.

If you read the entire chapters 1 Cor 12 - 14 with this in mind, I believe it will clear up a lot of confusion. There are two different types of tongues. One is for public ministry (which must be interpreted) and the other is for private use in personal prayer (and is available to everyone). Hopefully this explanation will help make sense of these confusing passages.

HOLY UTTERANCE IS IMPORTANT

One thing that is vital to notice in Scripture is that all the way through both in the Old and New Testaments – there is a "holy utterance" that comes forth when the Spirit of God comes upon a person. If we look at the Old Testament prophets, we find that when the Holy Spirit fell on them they prophesied. That was the result. The Spirit brought forth a "holy utterance" from their lips.

Just to give one famous example, when the prophet Samuel was anointing Saul to be king, he told him, "You will meet a group of prophets coming down from the high place with a stringed instrument, a tambourine, a flute, and a harp before them; and they will be prophesying. Then the Spirit of the Lord will come upon you, and you will prophesy with them and be turned into another man" (1 Sam 10:5-6). And that is exactly what happened. When Saul met the group of prophets, the Bible says, "the Spirit of God came upon him, and he prophesied among them" (verse 10).

Of course, we see this exact same pattern in the Book of Acts also. When the Holy Spirit falls upon a person, the "holy utterance" of God pours forth from their lips. In Acts 19:6 we read that "the Holy Spirit came upon them, and they spoke with tongues and prophesied." In Acts 10:45-46 we read that "the Holy Spirit had been poured out on the Gentiles also. For they heard them speak with tongues and magnify God." And in Acts 2:4 we read that "they were all filled with the Holy Spirit and began to speak with other tongues, as the Spirit gave them utterance." There it is – "the Spirit gave them utterance."

But the wonderful thing about 'tongues' in the New Testament is that it does not go away. This is not just a one-off fleeting experience. It is something that abides and remains. Once you have received "tongues," you can pray to God using this holy utterance any time you wish. And of course, this is just one evidence that the Holy Spirit remains with us and in us – just as Jesus promised.

FLAKEY CHARISMANIA – A BIG PROBLEM

Sadly, one of the things that is causing great harm in the church today is the misuse of the gifts of the Holy Spirit and a chronic lack of discernment amongst some Spirit-filled believers. Just like the Corinthian church in Bible times, it seems that having the Holy Spirit is no guarantee of sound doctrine or behavior. This seems very strange to some people. They quite rightly ask, 'How can these Charismatics claim to have the Holy Spirit when they are caught up in such unholy and unbiblical things?'

Even though I have been involved with the Charismatic movement myself for over 25 years, I personally have less and less desire to be tarred with the "Charismatic" label. The movement has sadly lost its moorings in so many ways. From Prosperity preachers scamming money to conference-hoppers chasing "gold dust" & angel feathers, to false revivals and big leaders falling into gross sin – this is a movement that has gone tragically off the rails. And yet, God is still more than able to fill people with His true and pure Holy Spirit in our day - as in any other.

I often get people asking me who they can trust to "lay hands" on them and pray for them to be filled with the Holy Spirit today. I usually tell them to find some little Pentecostal Holiness or AOG or Foursquare Pentecostal fellowship and simply ask the pastor to pray for them. You can usually tell by attending just one meeting whether there is something weird or unbiblical about a group. If it seems pretty sound, then just go ask the pastor to pray for you – that you might be filled with the Spirit and speak in "tongues". Is tongues important? Yes – I believe it is. It is the 'holy utterance' of God.

WHAT ABOUT THOSE WHO DON'T SPEAK IN TONGUES?

Perhaps you have come across people who claim to have experienced the baptism of the Holy Spirit – and yet they've never spoken in tongues. I have come across people like that too, on occasion. Usually I will gently encourage them to seek God for this gift. You see, I am generally reluctant to accept something as a full "baptism of the Spirit" unless it is accompanied by a real 'utterance' of the Holy Spirit. This is a sign that God has "taken over" a person's mouth by His Spirit – and it is important – as we see all the way through Scripture.

However, I am never so completely dogmatic about it that I totally exclude the working of God in some other way. Is it possible for some people to receive this Spirit-baptism and yet resist "tongues"? I cannot discount this totally, although in my experience, people who are resistant toward 'tongues' are usually resistant toward the Holy Spirit as well. In effect, many of them are saying to God, "Please give me the gift of your Spirit, God, but I would like to pick and choose the way in which He comes." There is a certain lack of childlike surrender about this approach. And to such people God usually says, "If you won't accept my gift in my way, then don't expect to receive it at all."

However, it may be good to take a look at one of the classic accounts of Baptism of the Holy Spirit from church history. Below is the famous revivalist Charles Finney's description of his own baptism in the Spirit, which occurred the day he truly repented and totally surrendered his life to God:

"As I closed the door and turned around, my heart seemed to be liquid within me. All my feelings seemed to rise and flow out, and the cry of my heart was, "I want to pour my whole soul out to God." The intensity was so great that I rushed into the room behind the front office, to pray.

There was no fire and no light in the room, but it appeared to me as if it was perfectly light. As I went in and shut the door, it seemed like I met the Lord Jesus Christ face to face. It seemed to me that I saw Him as I would see any other man. He said nothing, but looked at me in a way that broke me right down at his feet. I poured out my soul to Him. I wept aloud like a child, and made whatever confessions I could. It seemed to me that I bathed His feet with my tears; and yet I had no distinct impression that I touched Him.

I must have continued this way for quite some time, but I was too absorbed to remember anything I said. I know that as soon as my mind became calm enough, I returned to the front office, and found that the fire was nearly burned out. But as I turned and was about to take a seat by the fire, I received a mighty baptism of the Holy Spirit. Without any expectation of it, without any thought in my mind that there was any such thing for me, the Holy Spirit descended upon me in a way that seemed to go through me, body and soul. It was like a wave of electricity, going through and through me. Indeed it seemed to come in waves and waves of liquid love. It seemed like the very breath of God. I remember distinctly that it seemed to fan me, like immense wings.

No words can express the wonderful love that filled my heart. I wept aloud with joy and love; I literally bellowed out the inexpressible floods of my heart. These waves came over me and over me, one after the other, until I cried out, "I will die if these waves continue." I said, "Lord, I cannot bear any more." Yet I had no fear of death. How long I continued in this state, with this baptism continuing to roll over me and go through me, I do not know. But I know it was late in the evening when a member of my choir - for I was the leader of the choir - came into the office to see me. He found me in this state of loud weeping, and said to me, "Mr. Finney, what's wrong?" I could not answer for some time. He then said, "Are you in pain?" I gathered myself up as best I could, and replied, "No, but so happy that I cannot live."" (Source – 'The Memoirs of Charles G. Finney').

What a glorious account of the moving of God upon a young man's life! Of course, you will notice that Finney does not specifically mention 'tongues' (this was the 1800's after all) – but he does say, "I literally bellowed out the inexpressible floods of my heart." What exactly he means by this we will never know.

RECEIVING TONGUES TODAY

It was only after the first Pentecostal Revival at Azusa Street in 1906 that the concept of 'tongues' seemed to be truly restored to the church. As Frank Bartleman noted, from then on those pioneers found that, "All who received this 'baptism' spoke in 'tongues.'" ('*Azusa Street,*' pg 62). And this became the basic Pentecostal position. As I said earlier, generally it is mine also.

Having said that, it does not mean that I believe in "forcing" tongues on people, or any such thing! This is a gift of grace. I have sometimes seen Christians being far too aggressive when praying for others to receive this gift. I believe this is counter-productive. People may just utter a few strange syllables to make others happy. We must never forget that the Holy Spirit is a gift from God. All we need to do is encourage people to focus on worshipping Jesus and accepting this gift as a little child. Tongues should be a natural 'flowing' out – not a "forced" response. I certainly believe in encouraging people to expect tongues, but not in such a way that it creates spurious "fake-outs" instead of the real thing. This is very important.

When I last visited Nigeria I heard about quite a large movement where the people are literally told to "copy" tongues from the leaders at the front. In other words, they do nothing more than precisely imitate the "baby sounds" that the leaders are making – calling it tongues! Of course this is far from the truth. Tongues are the "flowing out" of the utterance of the Spirit within us – like rivers of living water. And we need to encourage people to settle for nothing less.

However, there are some who are fearful of seeking the Holy Spirit or opening themselves up to His gifts. They are worried about what they might receive. This is a very common problem – especially with the mess that the Charismatic movement is in today.

But we must remember that Jesus specifically addressed this issue. In Luke 11:11-13 we read, "If a son asks for bread from any father among you, will he give him a stone? Or if he asks for a fish, will he give him a serpent instead of a fish?... If you then, being evil, know how to give good gifts to your children, how much more will your heavenly Father give the Holy Spirit to those who ask Him!" Notice that in this passage Jesus specifically addresses people's fear of "what they might receive." He is telling them to go for it! We cannot allow fear to hold us back from receiving everything that God has for us.

We have already spoken about the fact that there are many little Pentecostal fellowships all over the world today that would be perfectly fine places to go for the "laying on of hands" and prayer to receive the Holy Spirit. That is one option. But of course, seeking God by yourself at home for this gift is also a great thing to do. It may be more biblical to go for the "laying on of hands," but we must remember that God is a rewarder of those who "diligently seek Him." Deep repentance and total surrender are the keys – wherever you are. Some people receive at home – but probably more receive in meetings and fellowships, etc. So don't limit God, either way!

And getting filled with the Holy Spirit is not just a "one-time" event, either. We are to be continually filled with the Spirit, over and over again. We see this in both Acts and Ephesians (Acts 4:31, Eph 5:18).

So never stop seeking God to be more and more filled with His wonderful Holy Spirit!

CHAPTER THIRTEEN

TYPES AND SHADOWS

We stated earlier that there are many texts throughout the New Testament that give us additional proof and insight into the Bible way of becoming converted. Interestingly, a number of them use Old Testament "types and shadows" to make a point about today's New Covenant.

What do we mean by 'types and shadows'? Basically, it is when some physical event or practice from the Old Testament has a real, spiritual application in the New. For instance, the lamb that was slain during Passover in the Old Covenant is symbolic of the death of Christ in the New - and so on.

In Heb 10:1 and Col 2:16-17 the Bible describes the Old Testament as a "shadow" of the New. So there are many of these symbolic patterns and events in the Old Testament that have a spiritual equivalent that is totally "real" for us today. That was the 'shadow' back then, and now we have the real thing.

So let us take a look at some of these "types and shadows" that the Bible refers to when it is talking about conversion. Please complete the Bible Study below, where we look at the first of these:

BRIEF BIBLE STUDY

(a) Please READ 1 Peter 3:20-21. The type or 'shadow' from the Old Testament that is being used here is the story of Noah and the Ark. Peter says that Noah's family was "saved through water".

- 83 -

What does he say is the New Testament equivalent of this?

ANSWER - _____

(b) Do you find Peter's statement a little shocking here? If so, why?

ANSWER - _____

_____

(c) Do you feel his statement here fits with what we actually see in the Book of Acts?

ANSWER - _____

SIMILAR SYMBOLISM

Of course, there are many accounts in the Old Testament of people being "saved through water." This is quite a dominant theme if you think about it. Noah is an obvious example, but also Jonah spent three days and nights in the belly of the whale before being deposited on the shore to see Revival in Nineveh. And when it came time to enter the Promised Land, the children of Israel had to cross through the Jordan river – which God miraculously parted for them. (Josh 3:14-17).

There is also the account of Naaman the Syrian, a leper who was told by Elisha to wash himself seven times in the Jordan River – and he would be healed. Scripture tells us, "So he went down and dipped seven times in the Jordan, according to the saying of the man of God; and his flesh was restored like the flesh of a little child, and he was clean" (2 Kings 5:14).

Then of course, there is the miraculous escape of the children of Israel through the Red Sea – which we again know was supernaturally parted by God. Like Noah, this last example is referred to in the New Testament as a "type and shadow" of true conversion. Please complete the Bible Study below which takes a look at this:

MINI BIBLE STUDY - ESSENTIAL

As always, please look up each Scripture and write your answers to the questions below-

(a) Please READ 1 Cor 10:1-2. Again, this Scripture is using a "type and shadow" from the Old Testament to make a point about the New. If the Israelites were "baptized into Moses" in the 'cloud and in the sea' then what do you believe would be the New Testament equivalent?

ANSWER - _____

_____

(b) Please READ Gal 3:27. Do you think there is a connection between this verse and the passage that we just read in 1 Cor 10? If so, what?

ANSWER - _____

_____

(c) According to these passages and all that we've seen, how do you think we are "baptized into Christ"?

ANSWER - _____

(d) Please READ 1 Cor 12:13. According to this Scripture, how are we baptized into the "one body" of Christ?

ANSWER - _____

(e) Is it possible, then, to be part of this "one body" without being baptized in the Holy Spirit?

ANSWER - _____

SOME SHOCKING CONCLUSIONS

I don't know about you, but I find the implications of the above passages pretty stunning. And yet they are totally clear – and consistent with all that we have seen elsewhere. (And, in fact, with the entire totality of Scripture). When Paul writes that the children of Israel were baptized into Moses in the "cloud and in the sea" I simply cannot come to any other conclusion than that we today must be baptized into Christ "in water and the Spirit." Can you come up with anything else that makes sense?

There is evidence in Scripture that baptism in water and baptism in the Spirit are really two halves of a single baptism – a baptism "into Christ". There is a kind-of "death" on one hand, and a "resurrection" on the other. The two halves make a whole. And of course, this is a very important thing to keep in mind when seeing people converted the Bible way. We don't want to leave the job "half done".

Just as a side note, isn't it interesting that in two of the major water-related events in Scripture we find the figure of a DOVE playing a prominent role? The dove was seen with Noah after the deluge, and of course with Jesus after his baptism. Could this be mere coincidence – or is it yet another echo of the self-same pattern – the pattern of "water and the Spirit"?

CHAPTER FOURTEEN

REMISSION OF SINS & THE NEW BIRTH

Here is an interesting question that we have not yet looked at in any depth:- When we come to Christ for the first time, how do we obtain "remission of sins"? (The word 'remission' means forgiveness). How do we get our past sins forgiven? What does the Bible say?

Again, we need to be prepared to be a little shocked at what Scripture teaches on this issue. But actually, it is something that we have already brushed up against in our previous travels. All the Scriptures we are about to look at are ones we have looked at before. But this time we are looking for something a little different in each of them – the "remission of sins." Please complete the Bible Study below as we look into this topic:

BRIEF BIBLE STUDY

(a) Please READ Luke 3:3. What was John the Baptist preaching "for the remission of sins"?

ANSWER - _____

(b) Please READ Acts 19:3-5. This passage shows that Christian baptism is different from John's baptism. What do you think is different? Is it that one is simply for "repentance" while the other is a "burial" into the death of Christ? Please give your opinion:

ANSWER - _____

(c) Please READ Acts 2:38. This Scripture implies that two things are needed for the remission of sins. Please write out these two things below – exactly as they are written in this verse:

ANSWER - _____

_____

(d) Please READ Acts 22:16. When it says, "Arise and be baptized, and wash away your sins," do you think this tallies with what we have seen in the rest of the New Testament regarding "remission of sins"?

ANSWER - _____

FORGIVENESS & BEING 'BORN AGAIN'

It seems to me when I read the above Scriptures that preachers in the New Testament basically preached two requirements for the remission of sins. The first was Repentance and the second was Baptism. God had obviously led John the Baptist to lay the foundation for this. But the concept clearly continued into the New Covenant and the preaching of the apostles. Isn't this exactly what the Scriptures seem to show?

Thus, it appears that in conversion, Repentance and Baptism are taking care of the PAST, while the infilling of the Holy Spirit is taking care of the PRESENT and the FUTURE – i.e. The person's walk with God from that point on.

Of course, another aspect to all this that we have not yet looked at is the New Birth. Interestingly, although we use the term "born again" all the time in the modern church, it was not a term that was used a great deal in the New Testament. The main passage referring to it occurs when Jesus is talking to Nicodemus in John 3. But is there any evidence of baptism or receiving the Holy Spirit in these passages on the New Birth? That is exactly what we will be seeking to find out in the Bible Study below. Please complete it if you can:

BRIEF BIBLE STUDY

(a) Please READ John 3:3-7 and write out verse 5 below:

ANSWER - _____

_____

(b) Many people think that "born of water" means to be "born of a woman." Or is it perhaps referring to baptism? Please read the whole passage John 3:3-7 again. What is your opinion?

ANSWER - _____

(c) Please READ Titus 3:5-7. Verse 5 tells us that we are saved through two things. What are they?

ANSWER - _____

_____

(d) The "washing of regeneration" literally means the "washing of rebirth." Do you see a connection between this verse and John 3:5 that we looked at earlier? If so, what?

ANSWER - _____

_____

PERSISTANT PATTERNS

We have just looked at two of the main passages in the New Testament that discuss the New Birth in any depth. And again – just like elsewhere – we find evidence of baptism in both water and the Spirit seemingly coming to the fore. When John 3:5 speaks of being "born of water and the Spirit" and Titus 3:5 speaks of the "washing of regeneration and renewing of the Holy Spirit" it is hard to avoid the connection. By now, hopefully this will come as no surprise.

As we have seen, right the way through the New Testament there is evidence of a pattern of conversion that is totally foreign to the modern church. In what has to be the most staggering omission that it is possible to imagine, it seems that today's church doesn't even know how to get people "saved" the Bible way. Instead we have made up our own "cheap and easy" method to fit in with our "cheap and easy" age. It seems many of us can read clear scriptural statements that just go in one ear and out the other. We undertake studies of the book of Acts and somehow miss the glaring fact that their conversion process was utterly different from our own – not to mention virtually every other facet of early church life as well.

Instead of the 'Foundations' that were always laid in new converts' lives from the very beginning of their Christian experience, today we think we can pick our own. We can often be found preaching psychology, "motivation-speak" and humanism for a gospel, and a cheap "rote prayer" for a salvation process. No wonder the walls are falling down! False foundations create shaky structures. Every builder knows that. But we carry on regardless.

Isn't it obvious that the sad and tepid state of our Christianity today is directly related to the gospel we preach?

CONCLUSIONS THAT MUST BE DRAWN

We are now almost at the end of our biblical odyssey through the Scriptures in search of the conversion method of the apostles. I think it is safe to say that we have seen enough to draw some pretty strong conclusions.

We started by looking at the "six foundations" of Hebrews 6 – described in the Bible as the 'principles of the doctrine of Christ' – and asked ourselves if the apostles might use these foundations during the conversion process. It certainly seemed logical that they might do so.

We then went carefully through every major conversion that is detailed in the book of Acts – looking to see if it was these 'foundations' that were being used in converting people, or rather something different like the Sinner's Prayer or "Asking Jesus into one's heart." We saw very clearly that it was indeed the foundations of Repentance, Faith, Baptism, and Laying on of hands (for the infilling of the Holy Spirit) that the apostles used time and time again. And amazingly, the concept of a "salvation prayer" asking Jesus into your heart was never seen anywhere. In fact, nothing like it was ever found in the whole book of Acts. Yes, that's right – NOTHING LIKE IT.

This led to some pretty big questions, since the "little prayer" is THE method used by the modern church to get people 'saved' right around the globe. You have got to start asking some pretty significant questions when you discover that the church has gone all over the world preaching a salvation procedure that can't even be found in Scripture.

During our search we also noted that Jesus Himself had to go through baptism in both water and the Spirit at the very beginning of His own ministry. We also discovered that there was NEVER a time in Acts where a new convert was not BAPTIZED IMMEDIATELY. It was always done every time – without delay.

And as our journey took us on through the rest of the New Testament, we discovered that the Bible spoke of water-baptism as being a "death and burial" of the old life, a 'circumcision of the heart,' a "washing away" of sin, a baptism into Christ's death, and also strongly linked it with the 'remission of sins' and more. All of this was right there in black and white, confirmed time and time again. And when baptism in water was combined with baptism in the Spirit we found strong linkages with the New Birth and being "baptized into Christ" (and His body). We also noted the fact that when the Holy Spirit comes upon a person, then "holy utterance" should result. Without this powerful infusion of the Holy Spirit, it seems the true Christian life is basically impossible to live out – according to Scripture.

This pattern of "water and the Spirit" was confirmed over and over – not just by the examples in Acts and the life of Jesus and the writings of the apostles – but also by types & shadows from the Old Testament as well. The confirmations were everywhere.

And so there you have it, my friends. A conversion process that is utterly different from everything we see in the modern church. So whom are we to believe? Is it the Bible? Is it Jesus and the apostles? Or is it today's thoroughly lukewarm church?

THE END APPROACHES

Even though we are virtually at the end of our study on this topic, it really does not have to be the end. There is any amount of study you can do yourself to come to grips with this subject in a much deeper way. For instance, you can carefully read through the entire Book of Acts yourself, noting every conversion that you can find. Or you can do a study of every single use of the word "baptism" or 'Holy Spirit,' etc, in the whole New Testament. There are all kinds of studies you can undertake. I encourage you to do all this and more if you truly care about this topic. It really is that important.

Chapter Fifteen

CHALLENGING THE STATUS QUO

Of course, baptism in water and the Spirit are not the only things that confront our current way of doing things in the church. In fact, if we are honest, whichever way we turn we are confronted with disturbing challenges to our lukewarm ways. Whether it is the topic of "What is the Gospel?" or 'How is real Christianity to be lived out?' or "What does it really mean to be a disciple of Jesus?" – these are gigantic questions and today we clearly have mostly-wrong answers. I mean, what on earth do we think we are playing at? Do we have no fear of the Lord? What are we teaching? What are we doing? Does anyone care if so much of it is wrong?

Is it OK for the modern evangelical church to be "compassing land and sea" making converts that are truly no converts at all? What do you think God is going to do to the preachers who spend their lives teaching such things? Aren't some of these topics the most serious topics that it is possible to discuss? How could it be that we have got such extreme basics so wrong for so long?

Is it any wonder that the world no longer comes to us for answers when we don't even know the basics of our own faith? Is it any wonder that the church has such a credibility problem when we are so unlike the Bible in so many ways?

The patterns that we have been looking at in this book go much deeper than just "salvation methods" or procedures. They strike at the heart of everything the modern church is, and everything she is doing. Because so much of it is utterly unbiblical. Salvation is only the beginning of it. But surely it has to be the most vital of them all.

If we are not getting people saved the Bible way, then are we getting them saved at all? If we are not turning people into disciples like the Biblical disciples, then are we actually making disciples at all? And if the modern church is nothing like the church of the Bible, then is it Christ's church at all? What are we basing everything on, if it's not the Scriptures? What on earth happened to the purity, the power and the pattern of the early church – and why aren't we desperate to recover it?

The fact that the "principles of the doctrine of Christ" and the basic foundations of the faith are being left begging on the side of the road is terrible enough, but it is not the whole story. The brutal fact is that not enough people care about Truth any more, not enough people agonize about the state of Christianity any more, not enough people will lay down their lives for the true gospel any more. And so we are left paupers. We desperately need a "Greater Reformation."

We truly think we are 'rich and increased with goods and have need of nothing' in today's church. But we do not realize that we are "wretched, miserable, poor, blind and naked" in all the ways that really matter. It is just like Jesus said. The church needs a total "revolution."

This is the deeper meaning of the missing patterns in our "cheap and easy" salvation method today. They are symptomatic of a far greater disease. Selfishness, neglect, convenience, apathy and a degrading lack of courage and leadership is taking a frightening toll. The world awaits the "prophets and wise men" who will stand up and fight for truth again in our day. I wonder who will heed such a mighty call?

REACTIONS – BOTH GOOD AND BAD

For some, the topics that we have been discussing in this book are too close to the bone. The implications are too hard to take. Even if they can see the validity of much that we present – and the fact that the Scriptures seem so clear on much of it – it is easier to dismiss the whole thing out of hand than to have to deal with the consequences. As Winston Churchill once famously said, "Men occasionally stumble over the truth, but most of them pick themselves up and hurry off as if nothing ever happened." But when we consider that this particular truth that we are discussing is actually a matter of ETERNAL CONSEQUENCE, surely we cannot afford to shrink from it in such a way? Surely we have to confront it and examine it honestly and deal with it straightforwardly?

All I am advocating and all I have ever advocated is literally taking the Scriptures at face value and putting them into practice exactly as they are written. Especially if there is overwhelming evidence that we see again and again and again. Can we afford to do otherwise? The Bible promises a "stricter" judgment to those who teach the word. We cannot risk preaching anything less than the whole truth as it has been revealed. We place ourselves in great danger if we do.

But I have seen all kinds of reactions to what I think are very plain scriptural truths over the years.

When I first wrote an article on this topic back in the 1990s, I got a huge mix of responses. Many were positive but others were quite angry. Several readers accused me of being "legalistic" and 'majoring on minor points'. I have to say I really cannot see this. I know that some doctrine is "straining at gnats" while some is really crucial. I believe this issue falls into the second category. I cannot believe that anything related to SALVATION is a minor thing.

There were also other readers who accused me of being "too literal"! (I had to laugh over this). Now these are foundational Bible truths we are talking about here, aren't they? Too literal? What on earth else should we be?

FACING THESE TRUTHS HEAD-ON

The fact is, I was deeply challenged myself when I first came face-to-face with this whole topic some years ago. I think these truths are very apparent when you study them, but I was blind to them for years. I was amongst those who gave out tracts like 'The Four Spiritual Laws' and led people in the "sinner's prayer".

I am not ashamed that I used to do these things. It was all I knew at the time. But I was certainly shocked to discover how much of the basic gospel I was leaving out. Like me, there are a number of you who will have to "search the Scriptures to see if these things be so" just as the Bereans did. Believe me, I fought these truths for months before I simply ran out of corners to back into. I knew the implications were huge and I just did not want to face them. But there they were in black and white. And this is not a trivial matter. These are key gospel truths that we are talking about here.

Just think how many thousands of believers around the world today have received the Holy Spirit (including 'tongues') but have simply not bothered getting baptized. I myself have come across many people in this exact position. I think it's terrible, and I believe God does too. Not to mention all the believers who still have not been baptized in the Holy Spirit. Don't you think God's heart aches over all this? Why do people ignore His commands? Our church traditions and habitual patterns have a lot to answer for in this area. This has got to change, my friends. And I believe it will only change when the underlying doctrines are challenged. But if I am right, the devil will fight this all the way. He likes anything that leaves believers impoverished or still chained up in any way. This really is crucial doctrine, otherwise I simply would not bother with it. I have really stuck my neck on the line and risked my reputation over this. And I do not do so lightly.

SOME ENCOURAGING REPLIES

One good thing about this topic is that none of it is about our own "opinions". It is about what the SCRIPTURES CLEARLY SAY. All we need to do is literally "let the Bible speak" on this matter and simply go along with what it says. Below are several interesting replies that I got from readers who had genuinely searched out these Scriptures for themselves and allowed the Bible to speak to them:

Rachel H. writes:

I want to thank you so much for your article on Lie # 1 - "Ask Jesus Into Our Heart". I was raised in a Baptist church also, so this is all new to me. I was sceptical at first, but I looked up every single verse in that article, and I have to say, WOW! I never knew that baptism played such an important role in becoming a Christian! I was baptized at a young age, but that was only because I had said that famous short prayer to accept Jesus into my heart, and attended the baptismal preparation classes!

I know that now, 13 years later, its time to be truly baptized. You covered every area, most of which I have never even known about, thank you so much!

I would also like to share something that God had revealed to me a couple of months ago about churches and the body of Christ. It started after I read a book about a revival that had taken place in Africa in the 50's. The key factor to their revival was REPENTANCE. When the people realized that Jesus had died for their sins, and they truly believed, they began repenting, confessing sins out loud, in front of large groups of people!

They weren't doing it for show, many times they were crying and moaning, sickened at their own sins but desperate to get it out. There was such a spirit of conviction there, that some of the people, as poor as they were, began repaying money that they had stolen years before that, or giving back eggs and animals that they had wrongfully taken. They were asking for forgiveness from other people left and right for things they had thought or said in anger and hate. Some of the people tried to keep their sins in, and they actually got physically sick until that sin was confessed. Some of the sins were more serious, but sin is sin to God, right?

What God revealed to me about churches is that everyone has some hidden sin that they don't want anyone to know about. Even the pastors and elders are hiding sin that they don't want to share, because, of course, they don't want to be looked down upon! God showed me that people need to confess their sins, they need to be truly repentant of them for there to be any kind of revival.

Pastor David K. writes:

Bro Andrew Strom, thank you for your response on... "ASK JESUS into our Heart".

You have opened my eyes on this one. I have read your article line by line and verse by verse. You have turned my heart... I see your position and on this point concede, I have been trained more by tradition than by the Word.
-Sincerely, Pastor David K.

Ian writes:

Having just returned from India I must make the following observations re- salvation.

To be a Christian in the churches that I ministered in means a turning away from the old gods and destroying of all idols. They regard people as seekers of truth at this stage, but its not until they are Baptised in Water which is usually followed by an infilling of the Holy Spirit that they are regarded as Christian. I want to tell you that there is a tremendous cost to being publicly baptised. Often it is accompanied by a separation of family members who refuse to accept that they have become Christians. The truth is that if a Hindu comes to Church He is not persecuted but the moment a decision is made to be baptised "all Hell" breaks loose. Because what is happening is more than symbolic, it is an act of covenant. A demonstration of alliegance to a Kingdom.

Brian J. writes:

Rev. David Pawson from England has written a book and done a video, both entitled "The Normal Christian Birth"

Both are in line with your position. David speaks of repentance towards God, faith in Jesus, baptism in water and the infilling of the

Holy Spirit as the steps involved in the "Normal Christian Birth", based on the accounts in the Book of Acts.

Anchor Recordings summarise it as follows: "So often, spiritual disease can be traced back to an inadequate initiation into the Kingdom. A better birth means greater growth in a healthy Christian life. David Pawson discusses some crucial and controversial biblical texts, challenging many traditional interpretations. He questions the adequacy of the typical "'sinners prayer" approach and gives practical tips on helping potential disciples to repent, believe, be baptised and receive the Holy Spirit. 326 pages"

Perhaps those who argue against might like to read the book or get hold of the video themselves. In the UK both are available from- http://www.anchor-recordings.com/ [also Amazon too, I believe – ed].

CHAPTER SIXTEEN

GETTING THE CHURCH SAVED

At the beginning of this book we quoted an evangelical pastor in America as doubting that more than 5% of his congregation were truly saved. We also quoted Leonard Ravenhill who said that, "I doubt that more than two percent of professing Christians in the United States are truly born again."

It is an interesting fact that two of the greatest Revival preachers in history, John Wesley and George Whitefield, both had sermons that they regularly preached entitled "The Almost Christian." Of course, none of this had anything to do with Baptism or the like. It was simply aimed at the fact that so few "church-going" people demonstrated the fruits of being genuinely saved. And these 'Almost Christians' desperately needed to be shown the peril of their position – and to become truly converted. So often, classic Revival preaching was aimed at people like these.

I believe this is something that we need to look at as well – quite apart from any discussion of "the foundations" or the other things we have been discussing in this book. Because it is very possible to be doing all the right things, saying all the right things, and seemingly even exhibiting signs of the Holy Spirit – and yet not be right with God deep within.

The 'Almost Christian' is someone who knows how to talk, act and sing just like the real McCoy. They are experts at "putting on a show." There is no doubt that they have been baptized. Some of them even speak in tongues. They will quite often attend every church meeting, song service or prayer meeting that is going. They may even tithe and raise their hands during the singing. They certainly know how to greet people with a warm smile and a hug and a "God bless you." But deep inside there is something not quite right. There is sin, there is compromise, there is lack of a deep relationship with God. And all around the world, in their millions upon millions, there are "Almost Christians" sitting in churches every Sunday putting their best face on things. And it is a tragedy almost beyond imagining. We have got to preach heart-searching messages that will get these people saved!

FRIGHTENING SCRIPTURES

One of the scariest passages in the Bible is found in Matthew 7:21-23- "Not everyone who says to Me, 'Lord, Lord,' shall enter the kingdom of heaven, but he who does the will of My Father in heaven. Many will say to Me in that day, 'Lord, Lord, have we not prophesied in Your name, cast out demons in Your name, and done many wonders in Your name?' And then I will declare to them, 'I never knew you; Depart from Me, you who practice lawlessness!'"

Here we see people who call Jesus "Lord" and work miracles in His name – yet He does not truly 'know' them – and on Judgment day they will be cast away from His presence. These are clearly believers who are quite dedicated, yet there is seemingly sin in their lives that is distancing them from a holy God.

Many people today simply have not grasped just how HOLY God is. Even in the church, God's holiness is hardly preached about any more. Of course, this is one of our greatest problems.

The only characteristic of God that is repeated three times together in Scripture (for emphasis) is the word "Holy." God is so holy that it is not enough merely to say the word once. Only three times will do. And this is the only characteristic of God that the angels are crying out over His throne day and night – throughout all eternity. "Holy, holy, holy, Lord God almighty." We see this both in the Old Testament and the New.

God is an utterly "holy" God and He cannot live with that which is unholy. Many think that God is so forgiving that He will live happily with unholiness forever in His presence. They know that they are unholy inside, but they think (wrongly) that God will be happy to live with them anyhow. What they do not realize is that God's holiness will not allow Him to live with sin. In fact the very word "holy" means 'set apart'. God is utterly "set apart" from sin. The only way to live in His presence forever is to be utterly cleansed and made white inside by the blood of Jesus – washing us inside out. And if we have not allowed God to do this transforming work deep in our lives then we have no chance.

A lot of people are going to be very shocked on Judgment Day, thinking that God is only forgiving, loving and kind – and that He'll let unholy people live with Him for all eternity. They will be terribly surprised when He throws them into "outer darkness, where there is weeping and gnashing of teeth." God simply cannot live with the darkness that is hidden inside their lives. The Bible makes this very clear. That is why Jesus had to die for our sins. It was the only way we could be washed clean – so that we could live with God forever. Only those wearing pure white "robes" on the inside can live with a holy God. That is clearly what the Scriptures show. Clean white robes – washed in the blood of Jesus.

Are YOU in possession of robes like these, my friend? Is your conscience utterly clean before God? As the old hymn says, "Are your garments spotless, are they white as snow, are you washed in the blood of the lamb?"

So many people are going to be shocked on Judgment Day because they tried to get into the "wedding feast" wearing the wrong robes – or they tried to appear before a holy God with "spots" all over their garments. Please make sure this is not you, my friend.

THE FEAR OF THE LORD

As we saw earlier in this book, the last two Foundations found in Hebrews 6 are 'Resurrection from the dead' and "Eternal

Judgment." So I guess it is fitting that we close this book talking about these two things. The fact is, unless the gospel that we preach emphasizes both of them, then it is no full gospel at all. The fact that every human being will be raised from the dead to stand before the great white throne of God's judgment is something that we cannot leave out. Because unless people hear about God's wrath and holiness and judgment, they simply cannot understand what they need to be "saved" from. Most people today have never heard a gospel that tells them to 'flee from the wrath to come.' They have never heard that Judgment Day will be a day of terror for so many. And because of this, they simply do not understand salvation itself.

If I do not know the depths of what I am being "saved" from, then I have never heard the true gospel. It is as simple as that.

In all my studies of what the apostles and the old Revivalists used to preach, this is the most glaring difference to the tepid gospel of today. God's servants of old preached a piercing word that was totally designed to convict people of "sin, righteousness and judgment." Today's preachers don't do this, and therefore they don't see the same results. No conviction of sin, no deep repentance. Little wonder that the church is so lukewarm when this deep work has never taken place in their hearts. It is totally essential.

A lot of people simply don't realize that this age of "grace" ends on Judgment Day. In fact, the Bible clearly shows that God will be very angry on that day. This is what the word "wrath" means. It means the 'fierce anger' of the Lord. Even though God is so merciful in saving people today, that era ends when Judgment Day begins.

Here is what the Scriptures say: "I saw a great white throne, and Him who sat on it, from whose face the earth and the heaven fled away. And there was found no place for them. And I saw the dead, small and great, stand before God, and books were opened" (Rev 20:11-12).

As we see here, when the earth and the heavens take one look at God's face on Judgment Day, they simply "flee" away as fast as they can. So what do you think mere humans like you and I are going to feel like doing?

The Scripture goes on to say that "the dead were judged according to their works, by the things which were written in the books... And anyone not found written in the Book of Life was cast into the lake of fire" (Rev 20:12-15).

Of course, this is the very essence of "eternal judgment" which Hebrews 6 tells us is one of the Foundations that must be laid in every believer's life. An understanding of Judgment and the fear of the Lord is essential to progressing in the faith. You cannot comprehend the depths of God's mercy unless you see the depths of danger that sin has placed you in. You cannot comprehend the depths of God's love, grace or forgiveness until you see the depths of 'lostness' and wrath that you have been under. "He that is forgiven much, loves much."

HOW TO TRULY PREACH THE GOSPEL

One of the most important things that we see when we study the preaching of the apostles and the old Revivalists is that "bringing conviction" was often uppermost in their mind. They knew that for the word to go deep enough and bring forth lasting fruit, their preaching had to be very piercing and heart-searching. Over and over again we see this from the great preachers – all the way through history. The first step was always to bring people to deep Repentance. Then everything else would follow. Repentance was their huge aim so much of the time. And it has to be ours too, if we want to see results like theirs.

Of course, this is the exact reason why the old Revivalists used to preach on "sin, righteousness and judgment": They knew that Jesus had specifically stated that the Holy Spirit would CONVICT of these very things - "sin, righteousness and judgment"! (Jn 16:8). The whole purpose of their preaching was to unleash the convicting power of the Holy Spirit upon their hearers. They aimed to thoroughly awaken the consciences of the people. Welsh Revivalist Humphrey Jones once urged a young preacher: "...to preach with severity and conviction; aiming continually at the conscience; charging the people with their sins to their very face; having no regard for men's good or bad opinions; and avoiding the exhibition of self during the delivery of your sermon." Now THAT is Revival preaching! And it is so often what we see in Acts also.

When the apostle Paul preached the gospel fearlessly to governor Felix, the record tells us: "Now as he reasoned about righteousness, self-control, and the judgment to come, FELIX WAS AFRAID..." (Acts 24:25). Notice what Paul was preaching on! And as we saw earlier, on the day of Pentecost it was Peter accusing the Jews to their very faces of 'crucifying the Messiah' that caused them to be cut to the heart, and to cry out, "Men and brethren, what shall we do?" (Acts 2:36).

And when Stephen was preaching (Acts 7), what was it that caused the religious Jews to be "cut to the heart" and to "gnash at him with their teeth"? It was Stephen fearlessly accusing them of killing the "Just One, of whom you now have become the betrayers and murderers" (v 52). No wonder they wanted to stone him!

Paul said, "God will judge the secrets of men by Jesus Christ according to my gospel" (Rom 2:16). Here Paul very clearly tells us that preaching about Judgment Day was part of his gospel.

But it is not just that these master preachers emphasized Judgment Day and the "wages of sin." It was the WAY they did it. The whole point was "maximum conviction" – maximum piercing of the heart – maximum impact. And this involved being truly searching, truly bold and truly fearless. Tell me, where will God find courageous preachers like this in our own day? Preachers who don't care about 'reputation'? Preachers of confrontation and conviction, who "cry aloud and spare not" even in the face of popular opinion?

Of course, the anointing of the Holy Spirit was all-important to these men. They would soak the whole thing in prayer for hours before delivering the word. Without the Holy Spirit they were nothing – and they knew it. They would wield God's word not as some kind of blunt weapon to bludgeon people with, but rather as an incisive, precision instrument by the power of the Spirit. A "sharp, two-edged sword", penetrating deep into men's hearts, exposing hidden sins, motives and desires, and bringing true Godly sorrow and deep repentance. What these preachers were looking for was a "broken heart and a contrite spirit" – for only then could they be sure that the resulting repentance would be both truly deep and truly lasting.

And so it must be again if we want to preach like the apostles in our own day.

LEADING SOMEONE TO REPENTANCE

The question may arise at this point – how then do we lead someone to repentance before God? What do we tell them to do?

Well, of course, we don't want them just praying some little "rote prayer" that we have made up on their behalf! So what do we tell them instead? Simply to talk to God and confess any sins that come to their mind one-by-one to Him – with genuine godly sorrow. And also to utterly and completely SURRENDER every part of their life to Him – without reserve. Deep confession and surrender are the very essence of what Repentance is all about.

And after they have prayed to God very simply in this way, we need to take them and baptize them – and then pray for them to be filled with the Holy Spirit! It's as simple as that.

A PERSONAL REVIVAL

So does this apply to the "Almost Christians" as well – the ones who are sitting in church every week thinking they are saved when they are not? Yes – certainly! They need a very similar message. In fact, a lot of Revivals have begun with the conviction of the church people first. In past Awakenings the Revivalists would aim many of their most piercing sermons at the believers – knowing that if they could become truly and deeply transformed then it would affect everything else. True Revival almost always begins with the church. And confession of sin is a huge part of it. A lot of these 'Almost Christians' sitting in church can experience "personal Revival" just through deep confession and repentance towards God.

One of the things I often encourage even mature believers to do is to "make a list" of anything in their life that may be a problem between them and God. It sounds so simple, but it is often amazing the powerful transformation that can come into a Christian's life just by praying through a simple list like that and repenting for each thing one by one. It sounds "too simple" so a lot of people don't bother doing it. But anyone – young or old – can experience a "personal Revival" like this. A 15-year-old girl once sent me the following testimony:

"Bro. Andrew...
I am about to be 15 and my entire life I thought I was saved. I've grown up in a Christian home. I knew the word and I heard pretty correct things all my life and thought I was OK because I "asked Jesus to come into my heart" when I was 3 and I was baptized around 11. I believe God did something in me. I've spoken in tongues since I was about 4 ½.

We, as a church body, had just come out of the "building" and began to meet in houses in January of this year - even then I thought for sure this made everything right. I had gotten a hold of your teaching "How to Experience Personal Revival". I had listened to it about 10 times and thought it was great. Well on June 1st after talking to one of my very close friends about her experience with making a list like you said, I decided to take notes. Earlier that week I had begun to have these weird questions like, "Am I REALLY saved?"

Well, I took notes on that teaching and I'm telling you, I HEARD what you said. My heart heard it. Not just my ears. It was like a massive revelation – like an entire new gospel I had never heard before. You made a comment, "If you're not living in revived Christianity, what makes you think you're living in Christianity?" The more I thought about it, the more I realized that I had never been truly "saved".

I never experienced the first 3 weeks of being saved. I began to ask myself, "Why am I not walking with God like Adam did? Why don't I have that fear of the Lord? Am I even saved?" I thought about when it says that the people said, "LORD, LORD, we cast out demons, we spoke in tongues..." And it was like a light went off and I knew that I was not saved. I always thought that the battle and the race and the struggle was against sin and fighting temptation.

My whole life I had struggled with sin thinking that I had repented of it only to find myself the next day repenting of it again. It wasn't true repentance! TO CHANGE THE WAY YOU THINK. I had made everything so complicated! The simplicity of the gospel is so alive in my heart and mind. Anyway, it was like I got a small understanding of the holiness of God and he was someone I had never met before. I made a list like you said, and I poured my heart out to this holy God and asked him to take the biggest search light he had and show me anything that was displeasing to him and I repented of it immediately. After I did that I felt utterly different. Like a weight I had had my entire life that I didn't even know about was gone. It's like the sky is bluer and the grass is greener and the birds sing louder just because I know the true Jesus. I know that this is real. It's not like before. I woke up the next morning and it was still there. And the next, it was still there, and last week – it was still there!

It's so simple and my entire life I've believed, whether I've said it or not, in an American Jesus who would just let my sin pass on by. I am utterly ecstatic. I know I'm different! I look at the word and the things that I've underlined and highlighted with 4 different colors mean something completely different now. This past Sunday I actually got baptized in my next door neighbor's backyard. -All I want to do is approach my holy God with only the holiness He can give. And walk completely and utterly transparent before Him..."

PREACH ALL THE FOUNDATIONS!

There is no question that deep Repentance is the key to all the rest – and therefore must be majored on in our preaching today – just like the apostles and revivalists used to do. But I believe that what God is looking for is preachers who will preach ALL the basic foundations that we find in the New Testament – not just Repentance.

Even if you do not fully agree with every conclusion we have reached in this book, one thing we can all agree on is what the apostles actually DID when dealing with new converts. They clearly believed in seeing them Repent immediately, be Baptized immediately, and be filled with the Holy Spirit immediately. And who are we to do any different?

Another thing we cannot deny is that the "six foundations" of Hebrews 6 surely have to be restored to modern preaching in all their fullness. Clearly God does not want a church in any age that is missing out on the Foundations! And so we are left with the fact that we HAVE to start doing things differently in the modern church. Our cheap little "rote prayers" have to be left behind, and the full Foundations restored instead.

My great hope is that in these last days we can come full circle – back to the ways of the early church in all her fullness – with preachers who know how to preach piercingly by the Spirit and see people "cut to the heart." And when they are asked, "What shall we do?" they cry, "Repent, be baptized, and you shall receive the gift of the Holy Spirit" – just like the apostles in Acts used to do. I believe God is awaiting a new generation of preachers who will boldly proclaim the full gospel and who stand for the purity, the pattern and the power of the early church. Tell me, friend, might you be one of these?

VISIT OUR WEBSITE-

WWW.REVIVALSCHOOL.COM

= SHOCKING BIBLE STUDY =

IS THE "SINNER'S PRAYER" REALLY IN THE BIBLE?

(1) Welcome to a Bible Study that may surprise and even shock you! (As it does with a lot of people). If you want to get the most out of it, please write your answers to each question below.

(2) As you read each of the Bible passages, please answer each question-

(a) Please READ Heb 6:1-2. Then write out the "six foundations" below (numbering them)-

ANSWER -

How important do you think these six things are?

ANSWER -

What words does verse 1 use to describe these six things?

ANSWER -

Before we continue, let us talk briefly about Repentance and Faith, since these are such crucial things in any true conversion. What is Repentance? It is a "turning away" from sin involving 'Godly sorrow', confession to God and a real heart-change. What is genuine Faith? It is a simple childlike belief and trust in Christ's righteousness - not our own - to justify us before God and save us. Both of these things are clearly totally essential to salvation. But what about the other Foundations?

(b) One major thing that we are looking at in this section is whether or not the early church used the "sinner's prayer" to lead people to the Lord - or whether they used the FOUNDATIONS instead. What exactly did the apostles tell people to do to become truly converted? Did they ever use the "sinner's prayer"? If not, what did they use instead?

The book of Acts is probably the best place to start in answering these questions, as it is the only book where we actually see thousands upon thousands of people becoming converted.

READ Acts 2:37-38. What were the 3 things that Peter told the people to DO in response to the gospel? (Please number them)-

ANSWER -

Please read on through verse 41. Do we see any signs of the people saying a "sinner's prayer" or giving their "heart to the Lord" like we do today?

ANSWER -

How soon did they baptize them?

ANSWER -

(c) READ Acts 8:12-17. Again, in this passage, do we see people "asking Jesus into their heart" or "praying a little prayer" like we do today?

ANSWER -

Again, there seemed to be 3 important elements in their response to the gospel. What were these 3 things?

ANSWER -

How soon did they baptize them?

ANSWER –

What was the "laying on of hands" used for?

ANSWER –

(d) READ Acts 10:44-48. Is the pattern here similar to what we have just seen in the other passages? In what way?

ANSWER -

Do you think these people may have already been godly, holiness-seeking people - even before Peter preached to them? Give reasons for your answer.

ANSWER -

How did the onlookers know that these people were filled with the Holy Spirit?

ANSWER -

Was it "optional" for them to be baptized?

ANSWER -

(e) READ Acts 11:15-18 and compare it with Acts 10:44-48 and also Acts 2:4. Does it seem that being "filled with", 'baptized with', or "receiving" the Holy Spirit may all refer to the same experience? Quote Scripture to back up your answer.

ANSWER -

Also, in light of these passages, do you think that the Spirit "coming upon" or "falling upon" someone is generally referring to this same type of experience?

ANSWER -

(f) READ Acts 19:1-6. Do we see any signs of people saying a "sinner's prayer" or giving their "heart to the Lord" in this passage?

ANSWER -

Do you think these people had already repented - even before Paul preached to them? Give reasons for your answer.

ANSWER -

Write out the "pattern" of what happened to these people when they responded to the gospel preached by Paul.

ANSWER -

Is it basically the same pattern that we have been seeing in the other passages?

ANSWER -

How could Paul tell that they had been filled with the Holy Spirit?

ANSWER -

(g) The conversion of Saul (who later became Paul) is recounted in Acts 9 and also Acts 22. Please READ Acts 9:1-18. Do we see (1) Repentance, (2) Baptism and (3) Receiving the Holy Spirit in this passage?

ANSWER -

In this and other passages, did it seem to matter too much what ORDER baptism or the infilling of the Spirit occurred? Give more than one scriptural example as proof of your answer.

ANSWER -

(h) Let us look again at how soon people were baptized in the Bible. Did they have to wait 6 weeks, 6 months - or was it immediate? Please READ Acts 16:25-33. At roughly what time of day were the Jailer and his family baptized?

ANSWER -

Does the above passage give the impression that baptism is very important? In what way?

ANSWER -

Please READ Acts 8:35-38. Do you think Philip spoke about baptism when he was preaching the gospel to the Eunuch? How can you tell?

ANSWER -

Based on these passages, and all that we have seen, how soon do you think we should baptize people?

ANSWER -

We have now looked at virtually EVERY conversion that is detailed in the entire book of Acts. At any time did we see anyone "asking Jesus into their heart" or repeating a "sinner's prayer" in order to become a Christian?

ANSWER -

After all that we have seen, do you think that when people ask "What should we do?", then our best answer might be the same as Peter's on the Day of Pentecost? Please WRITE OUT Acts 2:38 below-

ANSWER -

(i) Let us now seek to answer this question: Is water baptism mostly just an outward "SYMBOL" - or is there something powerful happening SPIRITUALLY in baptism?

Please READ Rom 6:3-8. According to this passage, what happens to our "old life" through baptism?

ANSWER -

Please READ Col 2:11-12. According to this passage, what is

happening inside of us when we are baptized?

ANSWER -

Please describe what the term "circumcision of the heart" means to you-

ANSWER -

Regarding the practice of 'sprinkling' little infants, the Greek word "baptizo" means to "dip or immerse" - not sprinkle - and the two passages we have just read describe baptism as a "burial". Therefore baptism surely has to be by "full immersion" under the water. Do you agree?

ANSWER -

And anyway, little infants are not old enough to "believe" the gospel first. Please READ Mark 16:15-16. Can a little baby "believe"? And therefore, according to this passage, should they be baptized?

ANSWER -

OBJECTIONS TO THE TEACHINGS ABOVE

There are several objections that people often raise when they hear this teaching. Often they are trying to defend the idea that all we need to do is "pray a little prayer" to become a true 'Bible Christian'. They do not want to admit that the scriptural pattern is (1) Repentance, (2) Baptism, and (3) Receiving the Holy Spirit. Below are some of the main objections that people seem to raise-

(a) "What about the Thief on the cross?" - OUR ANSWER: We believe in "death-bed" repentance, and this is certainly an example of that. But it should also be noted that this took place BEFORE the New Covenant truly began - before Jesus died and rose again - and before the Spirit was given at Pentecost. Therefore it is not a very good example for us to copy if we want to experience a full New Testament conversion.

(b) What about Romans 10 - which is so often quoted as a kind-of "formula" for becoming a Christian? - OUR ANSWER: Please READ Rom 10:9-13. The first question we must ask is- Is this passage meant to be an actual 'formula' for salvation? Is that the actual purpose of it? Please give your opinion.

ANSWER -

Secondly, it is a wonderful passage about FAITH - a very important topic. But who is it written to - believers or unbelievers? Who is likely to be reading the book of Romans? Might Rom 10 perhaps be written differently if it really was a "salvation formula" being written to unbelievers?

ANSWER -

Thirdly, when we look at the OVERWHELMING evidence on the side of "Repentance, Baptism & Receiving the Spirit" - and we look at the fact that we cannot find anyone in the whole Book of Acts simply "praying a prayer" for salvation - shouldn't we go with the overwhelming Bible way? Surely we have to look at what the "weight" of Scripture teaches - and go with that? Isn't this what we should always do in these situations - go with the overwhelming "weight" of Scripture? Please give your opinion.

ANSWER -

Fourthly, Rom 10 says that "Whosoever calls on the name of the Lord shall be saved". But perhaps we should ask ourselves- "When did Paul himself first 'call on the name of the Lord'?" When did this moment occur for him? Please READ Acts 22:16 and write below the actual words that Ananias spoke to him-

ANSWER -

As we can see from the above passage, the moment when Paul first "called on the name of the Lord" was actually IN BAPTISM. Do you find this significant?

ANSWER -

Ultimately, I do not find Rom 10 to be conclusive proof against our teachings - or for the idea of a "sinner's prayer". It does not make sense to take that meaning from it when the whole rest of the New Testament teaches something different.

(c) Many people ask, "What about the old Revivalists and Reformers from past centuries? The Christianity of their time did not involve Baptism by Immersion or being filled with the Holy Spirit. What about these heroes of old?"

OUR ANSWER: I actually believe that God has slowly been restoring His truths to the church bit by bit over the centuries, since the Great Reformation. If you look at history you will see that it started with "Justification by Faith" in the 1500's, then the "New Birth" and Sanctification, then Baptism by Immersion, then healing, then Baptism of the Spirit with 'tongues', etc, until today we have the opportunity to fully enter into virtually everything that the early church entered into - and powerful Spirit-filled Revivals are happening around the globe. The church has come full circle in many ways, but still I feel we need one last Great Reformation to fully restore all that was lost. It has taken a very long time for the church to emerge out of the dark ages, and there have been many "heroes" along the way. To me, men like Luther, Wesley, Whitefield, Finney, etc, are a great inspiration - and I write about them and preach about them all the time. But yes - they lived in an era when Christianity seemingly had less light than she does today. Thus I believe all the people of those times will be judged by the light that they walked in. It is as simple as that. I do not condemn them at all - in fact I admire many of those old preachers and learn as much from them as I can.

(d) "Do you believe in Baptismal Regeneration?" - OUR ANSWER: No! We certainly do NOT believe in Baptismal Regeneration - which is basically an old Catholic doctrine. All we are saying is simply that the Bible way of becoming converted seems to be through Faith, Repentance, Baptism and Receiving the Holy Spirit. It is quite different from what we have been taught to preach today, and I believe we are short-changing a lot of people. Don't you think this has to be one of the most important topics that Christians today could possibly discuss? Please comment.

ANSWER -

(e) "Couldn't this be seen as a kind-of Salvation by works?" - OUR ANSWER: Absolutely not! Where are the "works"? Is Faith a work? Is Repentance a 'work'? Is water-baptism a work? (It is quick, it happens only once, and the person does not even do it to themselves - so how can they be "working"?) Is baptism with the Holy Spirit a 'work'? In my opinion, none of these things are remotely like 'works' at all. Where is the "working" going on? Please give your opinion.

ANSWER -

(b) Have you ever heard the verse Rev 3:20 "Behold I stand at the door and knock..." being used out of context to get people to 'ask Jesus into their heart'? Does it surprise you how utterly out-of-context it is?

ANSWER -

(c) When Andrew Strom commented that he now baptizes "In the name of the Father, the Son & the Holy Spirit - in the name of Jesus Christ" - what was his reason for adding "In the name of Jesus Christ" onto the end?

ANSWER -

(4) Please look up the following Bible passages and answer the questions-

(a) READ 1 Cor 10:1-2. This Scripture is using a "type and shadow" from the Old Testament to make a point about the New. If the Israelites were "baptized into Moses" in the 'cloud and in the sea' then what do you believe would be the New Testament equivalent?

ANSWER -

(b) Please READ Gal 3:27. Do you think there is a connection between this verse and the passage that we just read (1 Cor 10:1-2)? If so, what?

ANSWER -

(b) Please READ 1 Peter 3:20-21. Again, there is a type and shadow from the Old Testament being used here - this time Noah and the Ark. Peter says that Noah's family was "saved through water". What does he say is the New Testament equivalent of this?

ANSWER -

(c) Please READ Titus 3:5-6 and compare it with John 3:5. There may or may not be a connection between these two passages. Do you think so, and if so, what is it?

ANSWER -

(d) Please READ Matt 28:19. In light of this verse, do you think it is possible to "make disciples" without baptizing them? Quote the Scripture to back up your answer.

ANSWER -

(e) We ourselves tend to hold to the classic Pentecostal position regarding "tongues" - that generally they are the 'initial evidence' of getting filled with the Holy Spirit that we expect to see. Please WRITE OUT the following verses-

Acts 2:4

ANSWER -

Acts 10:45-46

ANSWER -

Acts 19:6

ANSWER -

Acts 8:17-18

ANSWER -

Mark 16:17

ANSWER -

1 Cor 14:18

ANSWER -

Of course, this baptism of the Holy Spirit is a baptism of Holiness and Power and Love and Victory over sin - which are the big important things that we expect to see in a person's life after this experience. But we regard tongues as an important "initial evidence" of receiving the Holy Spirit. -And vital for ongoing prayer also. Paul said "I speak in tongues more than you all." So he obviously prayed in tongues a lot. Shouldn't we do likewise?

ANSWER -

(f) OBJECTIONS TO 'TONGUES'

Some people believe that the gifts of the Spirit are not for today at all. This seems rather a ridiculous argument to us, but we cannot go into it here. The objection that we find most common is that many believe tongues is only for "some" believers - and yet we believe that God desires ALL His children to have such a 'prayer-language'. The passage that seems to confuse people most is found in 1 Corinthians. Please READ 1 Cor 12:29-30. Because this passage asks "Are all apostles, are all prophets... Do all speak in tongues?" (to which the obvious answer is "No"), people are left thinking that tongues is only for 'some'. But what they fail to notice is that this passage is speaking about "ministry gifts" in the church. The whole passage is listing 'ministry-offices' that some are called to. And one of these is to "speak out publicly" in tongues during a church meeting - which must always have interpretation. Only certain people are called to do this. That is the point Paul is making. They have a special anointing to use tongues as a public ministry - which is not for everyone. But certainly he is not talking about the private "prayer language" that we believe Scripture shows is available to every believer. If you read the entire chapters 1 Cor 12 - 14 with this in mind, we believe it will clear up a lot of confusion. There are two different types of tongues. One is for public ministry (which must be interpreted) and the other is for private use in personal prayer (- available to everyone). Does this explanation make sense to you?

ANSWER -

(5) Having studied this topic so thoroughly, do you now have the desire to go out and see people Repent, be Baptized, and be Filled with the Holy Spirit? Is that the type of conversion you want to see happening from now on?

ANSWER -

(6) HOMEWORK: Please go to at least 3 of your friends and acquaintances. Gently and lovingly share these Scriptures with them and make sure that they have been baptized and filled with the Holy Spirit. (Please be gentle!)

(7) FURTHER HOMEWORK: For further study on this topic you can simply look up every Scripture on Baptism and also the Holy Spirit - as well as the other Foundations - in the whole New Testament. Please use an "exhaustive" concordance if you wish to do such a study.

Lightning Source UK Ltd.
Milton Keynes UK
UKOW042322041212

203165UK00001B/283/P